The Complete
Cast Iron
Dutch Oven
Cookbook

The Complete
Cast Iron
Dutch Oven
Cookbook

1000 Days of Easy Tantalizing Recipes for
the Most Versatile Pot in Your Kitchen

Beginners Edition

By Faney Marck

CONTENTS

CONCLUSION 87

INTRODUCTION

When cooking in a Dutch oven, which was originally known as a multi-cooker, we are using a large, heavy pot that can be used to prepare virtually any dish that we desire. Dutch ovens are characterized by a tight-fitting lid and thick sidewalls made of cast iron, making them particularly well suited for baking tasks. When it comes to Dutch oven cooking, those who have used one are well acquainted with the pot's ability to retain heat and the nonstick nature of its surface. An electric Dutch oven is simple to use and clean. It does not necessitate the use of any complicated techniques to accomplish either task. As a result, they are among the most convenient cooking appliances that we can use in various kitchen settings, whether indoor or outdoor. When it comes to camping, the Dutch oven is the best cookware appliance to have, and it is also widely regarded as one of the most versatile cookware appliances available on the market today. Dutch ovens are versatile cooking vessels that can be used for various tasks such as roasting, baking, frying, broiling, stewing, steaming, and more.

Cooking in a Dutch oven is the best alternative to cooking in a conventional oven. You can use them for cooking anything normally cooked in an oven or on the stove. Aside from that, another advantage of using a Dutch oven over other backpack ovens is that it takes up very little space in your pack and can be transported to wherever you need to use it. Cooking in a Dutch oven is typically intended to serve groups of 6-8 people. Still, the amount of food you prepare can be adjusted to meet your specific needs.

If the year 1492 is credited with discovering the Dutch oven, does this year conjure up any particular images for you? To be sure, the first Dutch oven ever made its way to North America for the first time, and some historians believe Christopher Columbus was the one who brought the cast-iron pot with him to the New World. If, on the other hand, the Dutch oven was responsible for Columbus' discovery, then why was it referred to as a Dutch invention in the first place? A trade between Dutch merchants and New England settlers and Indians in the 15th century resulted in the Dutch oven, which was used for baking bread and other baked goods.

When we search the internet for an exact translation of this term, it is best described as a roasting or frying pan. This is consistent with Dutch tradition. On the other hand, the Dutch design is a pot made of enameled steel that is used for frying meats and is currently available for purchase on the market. The modern form of the Dutch oven is lightweight and inexpensive, and it is suitable for use with natural gas, allowing it to be used for the first time in indoor kitchens for baking and cooking.

The history of Dutch ovens reveals that this cooking appliance has been in use since the 17th century. According to further research, the first Dutch ovens were primarily made of brass in the early nineteenth century. Initially, a high-quality pot with smooth surfaces was molded at the beginning of the Dutch oven-making process, which was later refined by the English to use clay and loam instead of clay and loam. Although the process of making Dutch ovens improved significantly over time, they were first used by homesteaders, ranchers, pioneers, and miners alike in the early nineteenth century. These days, stores are brimming with a diverse selection of Dutch oven brands that have become widely popular throughout the globe.

PART ONE: OVERVIEW

CHAPTER 1:

ALL YOU NEED TO KNOW ABOUT DUTCH OVENS

What Can the Dutch Oven Do?

Although a Dutch oven is basically a heavy container pot with a tight-fitting lid, this cast-iron pot can also be a wonderful gift for home chefs worldwide. It is possible to cook almost anything in a Dutch oven.

In this article, we'll discuss one-pot meals, such as Alfredo pasta with tomato sauce and other tomato-based soups; biscuits; chili; beef stew; casserole; and the preparation of individual ingredients, such as sauces and garnishes.

You can even cut down on cooking time when using a Dutch oven because the pot can be transferred directly from the stovetop to the oven without missing a beat. Many Dutch oven recipes allow you to combine all of your ingredients in a single mixing bowl.

Dutch ovens have been used for hundreds of years to cook a variety of foods. Nothing, not even the heavy metal in this monster bowl, will be able to maintain a reasonable temperature.

Before we get started, let's go over some of the important information you should be aware of.

There are hundreds of different Dutch oven variations available on the market, so it would be impossible for me to tell you which oven is best for your cooking preferences.

Because each type of oven is designed to cook in a different situation, I'll go over the various options, and you'll decide which one is best for you after you've reviewed them. It is important to choose a well-made oven when shopping for your new oven. Cooking is something I would never compromise on in terms of taste or quality!

The bail handle of an outdoor Dutch oven should be scrutinized if you're looking for one. This wire should be a heavy gauge wire and should be firmly connected to shaped tangs on the outside of the oven. Ovens with riveted tabs should be avoided.

The majority of oven handles are oriented in both directions against the side of the oven. Still, if you look closely, you can find some with a handle angled at 45 degrees on one leg.

In addition, the handle on the lid should be thoroughly inspected. A loop should be attached to both ends of the cover, and the center of the cover should be hollow to allow for easy locking and unlocking. Stay away from doors with a sturdy shaped tab for a handle on the inside of the door. A faulty lid will be extremely difficult to grasp and handle, especially when a large amount of coal is used. The loop layout provides significantly more control. A lip or ridge should be present around the outer edge of the lid.

The lip on the lid prevents the coal from falling out of the ashpan. Use the ridge-less version if you prefer, but it's difficult to keep the coal on the lid, and if you don't clean the ash from the lid every time you open the oven, you'll end up with ash and sand in your food.

The presence of a lip practically eliminates this problem. Even when the lid is completely loaded with ash and coals, it is relatively easy to remove.

The legs are another feature that should be carefully examined. Ovens with flat bottoms and ovens with four legs are available, but the most common type is three legs. The legs are essential for outdoor cooking because they raise the oven above the coals, allowing for better ventilation below.

The oven's flat bottom allows it to be set on rocks or steel tent pegs with little danger of tipping over. According to Murphy's law, it is best to leave the flat bottom ovens in the store or on the kitchen stove where they belong, rather than in the house.

In addition, look for a second handle attached to the lid or the top rim of the oven at the base.

Many ovens are available with a skillet-style handle that is attached to the lid of the oven. Although this appears to be a good idea, in theory, they are not providing adequate support in practice.

These handles also become a hindrance during the storage and packaging process. Fixe handles on the base of the oven must be avoided at all costs, even though I believe the theory behind these handles was to encourage the placement of the oven in a deep fireplace.

Bring a couple of red bricks with you to the store, and place them in an oven with this type of handle while you're there. You can then attempt to raise the pot using the handle. You'll quickly discover that the handle is completely ineffective. The weight of a loaded oven, weighing 20-25 pounds, can be a real wrist-breaker.

The only exception is a small tab on the upper lip of the oven that is about 1/2-1 inch deep and 2-3 inches long, which is often present. This tab makes it very simple to pour liquids from the oven, and the fact that it is so small has never caused any problems with storage or packaging. When someone mentions a "Dutch Oven," many people immediately think of cast iron. Still, Dutch ovens can also be made of aluminum or other lightweight materials. The weight of an aluminum oven is approximately 6-7 pounds, whereas the weight of a cast-iron oven is approximately 18 pounds.

Each type of material has its own set of advantages and disadvantages. The most obvious advantage of aluminum is its light weight, which is one pound lighter than steel. In addition, because aluminum does not rust, the only treatment required is a thorough cleaning with soap and water.

Aluminum tends to heat more quickly, requiring less preheating time. Still, it does not retain its heat for a long period after being removed from the coals. In addition, aluminum reflects more heat than cast iron. It will take more coals to reach and maintain a set temperature with aluminum.

With an aluminum Dutch Oven, you will also notice a greater degree of temperature variation on windy days. It is possible to overcome the majority of the disadvantages of aluminum in situations where weight is critical.

This type of temperature can be produced if the oven is placed directly on the coals or if there are many coals beneath the oven.

Other Things You Might Need

A reliable pair of leather gloves can save time around a fire and prove invaluable. A couple of work-style gloves are going to do that. Still, I suggest you look for a fire and safety supply house or store that sells fireplace accessories and find a couple of fire handling gloves.

The extra protection and efficiency far outweigh the few extra dollars that fire handling gloves cost. You'll have to weigh the standard for yourself against the higher price.

You are going to need a shovel. The typical garden shovel will be enough. It will be used to heat and raise the coals to the oven from the fire pit. The handle's style and length are up to you. The long-handled shovels are great on hikes and canoe trips but not practical for use with ovens.

While the short "army shovels are perfect for hiking and canoeing, they suffer from short handles, getting too close to the fire, and risking bums. A pair of hot pot pliers is another object that will prove worth its weight in gold.

CHAPTER 2:
TYPES OF DUTCH OVENS TO KNOW ABOUT

Camping

There are three legs to keep coals out, a wire bail handle for lifting the Dutch oven, and a slightly concave, rimmed cover to place the coals or briquettes on top and bottom of the pot. It improves the consistency of internal heat and allows the interior to function as an oven. Typically, these ovens were constructed entirely of bare cast iron. Cooking methods such as roasting, baking, stewing, frying, boiling, steaming, and many others can be accomplished quickly over a campfire using only one utensil, a Dutch oven, and little preparation time.

These and a slew of other options are very feasible, and in some cases, even simpler than doing so at home. With only a few exceptions, you'll be able to replicate your favorite home recipes using a Dutch oven over an open fire.

Modern

These Dutch ovens are designed to be used on the stove or in the oven and usually have a lipless top.

Like the unglazed ovens, many older types retained the handle, while others, like the enameled, had 2 handles of the ring. Traditional Dutch ovens consist of cast iron, cast aluminum, or ceramic.

Usually, there are 2 cooking methods used with the Modern Dutch oven.

The first method places the food in the Dutch oven's center.

In the second method, food is cooked in a second dish and then placed in the bottom of the Dutch oven on a trivet. The trivet's purpose is to lift the plate above the bottom of the oven to avoid burning.

Selecting/Buying a Dutch Oven

Camping Hardware stores and sporting goods stores are the most common places to find Dutch ovens. New Dutch ovens are available for purchase in supermarkets and cooking supply stores and can be used on the stovetop or in a traditional oven.

When purchasing a Dutch oven, it is important to consider the size, style, and shape required. The Dutch aluminum oven is popular among backpackers because it is lighter, rustproof, and does not require seasoning.

If you opt for an aluminum oven, be careful not to overheat it, as this can cause permanent damage to the baking pan.

Many people prefer cast-iron ovens because they heat more evenly and maintain their heat for a longer period.

Generally speaking, the costs are comparable.

Select the Dutch oven that best meets your requirements. Dutch ovens are also available in a variety of sizes and are labeled according to their size number.

The sizes, weights, and capacities of the various containers are listed in the table below.

Diameter	Weight	Capacity	Serving Capacity
8-inches	3 lbs.	2 quarts	2-4 people
10-inches	5.5 lbs.	4 quarts	4-6 people
12-inches	7.5 lbs.	6 quarts	6-10 people
14"	9.5 lbs.	8 quarts	10-12 people
16"	11 lbs.	10 quarts	13-15 people
18-inches	13 lbs.	12 quarts	16-18 people
20"	14.5 lb.	14 quarts	19-22 people

Dutch Oven Tools

There are a variety of Dutch oven gadgets available that are designed to make it easier to use your oven while cooking outdoors. One of the most useful tools is a long-handled hooked lid remover with a curved handle.

Such devices help to speed up the cooking process in an outdoor Dutch oven. No special equipment is required when cooking with a Dutch oven on the stovetop or in a conventional oven. Preparing your Oven is a simple process.

The only pretreatment required for aluminum is a thorough washing with soap and water before use. Many aluminum ovens are delivered with a protective covering easily removed with a quick rinse in the dishwasher.

If cast-iron ovens are properly maintained, they will last a lifetime. I know several Dutch ovens that belonged to their great grandmothers and date back to the 1800s or even further back.

Even though this book is geared toward Dutch ovens, any cast-iron skillet, grid, or similar item is subject to treatment and care instructions. No, the secret to cast-long iron's service life is not a mystery at all.

Regular and meticulous maintenance will ensure that the oven continues to operate for many years, beginning with the purchase date. Neither standard Dutch ovens are shipped with a protective coating, which should be removed before use.

To clean your new oven, you will need to use steel wool and a lot of elbow grease. Clean the oven thoroughly, blot it dry with a towel, and allow it to dry naturally. Pre-heating your kitchen oven to 3 509F would be an excellent time to do so while the dish is drying.

When it appears to be dry, place the Dutch oven on the center rack of the oven and leave the lid slightly ajar. Continue to heat the Dutch oven at a slow, steady rate until it is just barely too hot to touch with bare hands. This pre-heating process removes any remaining moisture from the metal and allows the pores to open.

Apply a thin layer of salt-free cooking oil to the dish's surface with a clean cloth or, ideally, a paper towel. You can use a variety of oils, including almond oil, olive oil, and vegetable oil. Tallow or lard will also work, but these animal fats have a tendency to break down during long periods of storage, making them unsuitable for use in traditional Dutch ovens during campouts.

To ensure that every inch of the oven, both inside and outside, is coated with oil, place the oven on the center rack with the lid slightly ajar. Preheat the oven to 3 509F for approximately 1 hour. The oil is transformed into a metal protective coating as a result of the baking process.

After baking, allow the oven to cool slowly. Once the handling has been proven to be safe, apply another thin oil coating. Repeat the baking and cooling process a second time.

When it is safe to treat it again, reapply a thin oil coating to the surface. Allow the oven to cool completely before using it again. This treatment calls for three layers of butter, two of which are poured on and one added warmly. The oven is now ready to be used or stored, depending on your preference.

Except in the case of rust formation or coating damage during storage or use, this pre-treatment procedure is only required once. Anything that has been baked on the surface will darken and turn black over time. Having a well-maintained and well-used oven, this darkening is a sign of that. The pre-treatment coating acts as a barrier between the metal surface and the moisture in the air. It effectively prevents the metal from rusting and coats the inside of the oven with a non-stick coating, making it ideal for baking. When properly maintained, this coating is as non-adhesive as most commercially applied coatings on the market.

Seasoning

First things first. Thoroughly wash the Dutch oven with soap and water and remove the protective cover. Afterward, either put it in your house or place it on a camp stove large enough to support its weight and let it thoroughly dry. When dry, preheat your regular oven to 450-5009F. Slightly brush the inside and outside of your Dutch oven with grease while the oven is preheating.

There are many different types of grease that you can use, from bacon to olive oil. Crisco in a tin is what I use. Do not use the scent of butter either.

When the oven is preheated, place a loosely greased Dutch oven in it and roast it for 1 hour. Remove the Dutch oven and let it cool. Don't turn off your oven.

The Dutch oven should now feel tacky. If it does, place it in the oven for another 30 minutes set for 300-3 5 09F. The process will take 2 hours.

Seasoning stops the iron from being absorbed into the cast iron and taint the way food tastes. Properly sealed pans have an easy-to-clean non-stick finish. With age and use, pans that are adequately cared for get better and better. There are 2 methods to season your Dutch oven. One is to thoroughly clean and dry, then apply half of the oil. Heat until the oil swirls to cover all the inside surfaces. Dispose of used oil and substitute with fresh oil.

Seasoning Your Dutch Oven Again

Consider the possibility that you did the unthinkable and left your Dutch oven out in the rain all winter, causing it to rust, or that you put it away and the grease went rancid.

There are two options available to you. You have two options: either buy a new oven or clean the one you have. It's simple to tell if your oven has become rancid: simply remove the lid and cover your nose while testing it out. If you start gagging after eating it, it's bad! You can also tell by the color of the pot, which turns yellow-orange and becomes gummy as it ages. Fill half of the oven with water, add a cup of vinegar and cook for 30 minutes on low heat.

Sprinkle some bath salts in there, and clean and re-season your oven. There are several methods for removing rust. Start with a steel wool pad, and if that doesn't work, soak the oven for a while. As a last resort, mix in a cup of apple cider vinegar and plenty of water, then cover with hay to prevent rot.

With these soaking methods, you must be patient and wait for the results. Sandblasting should only be used as a last resort. It is necessary to exercise caution when employing this strategy. Choose the sandblasting method that will be used. I was told that sand would dissolve the cast iron during the process, but glass beads would not. I called around, and it turns out that the places where car bodywork is also done clean Dutch ovens!

CHAPTER 3:
USEFUL TIPS AND TRICKS

Basic Don'ts

- Do not allow cast iron to sit in water or let water stand in or on it. Despite a durable coating, it will rust.

- Never use cast-iron soap. This will get into the metal pores, and it won't come out very quickly, but it will come back to taint your next meal. When soap is used unintentionally, the pre-treatment process should be extended to the oven, including removing the present coating.

- Do not put an empty cast-iron pan or oven over a fire. It can be better handled by aluminum and many other metals, but cast iron can crack or warp and destroy this.

- Do not heat cast-iron in a hurry. You will end up with burnt food or an oven or pan that is fried.

- Never put cold liquid in a pan or oven of scorching cast-iron. They're going to crack.

Cooking Tips

Dutch oven cooking can be done using a conventional oven or cooking top, a camp stove, a wood fire, or charcoal briquettes on the back porch.

Choose the best source of heat for your purposes. The wood fire and heat sources for briquets are the most challenging to use as heat control is difficult. The Dutch cast-iron oven retains the heat and uniformly cooks food. You have a more regulated heat source when using your conventional oven, stovetop, or camp stove.

A Dutch oven allows the cooking time to decrease because it retains the heat longer and takes less space to cook food.

Firewood Cooking

When you have a bank of hot coals around your campfire, wood campfires are ideal for cooking. Make a fire that is large enough to accommodate everyone. Ensure that there are enough coals to cover the top and bottom of the oven.

Managing the smoke produced by partially burned and burning materials is difficult because the heat required to thoroughly cook the food will be insufficiently maintained. With the help of a long-handled shovel, construct a large coal bank and a shallow pit. Using a shovel, spread a sheet of coal across the field. Place the oven in the coals and cover it with a layer of coals and soil to prevent it from overheating. Take care not to knock the lid off the shelf. When the food has finished cooking, scrape off any dirt or coals. Coals are typically extremely hot, and the only way to determine how hot the coals are is through personal experience.

Cooking With Briquettes

Light the briquettes, and let them get hot and grey. The oven's size will determine the number of necessary briquettes.

The general rule of thumb is to remember your Dutch oven's size. The number of coals on top of the oven is equal to the size. For the bottom, you are going to use half that number of briquettes.

Temperature

You can see that every briquette of charcoal is worth around 259F. Twenty coals will offer about 500 degrees.

Food Checking

Food can be checked by lifting the entire Dutch Oven out of the fire or coals and placing it on a flat surface. Remove the coals or briquettes from the fire pit and lift the lid straight up and down with the handle on the side of the pot.

Carefully remove the lid from the container and place it on a clean surface. Clean the area around the edge of the oven where the cover and the oven meet with a folded piece of paper towel.

Prepare the vegetables and meat by chopping them and adding moisture to see if they are cooked. Make an effort to remove the lid as soon as possible to avoid losing too much heat. If the coals are becoming too dry, they should be changed to remove some of the coals from the top or bottom of the oven.

If the food is taking longer to cook, increase the amount of hot coals used. Replacing the oven with a heat source and continuing to cook until the meal is completed.

Meat

It's beautiful to serve meats in a Dutch oven. They have a taste that you will never replicate using any other form of cooking.

Although the flavor is always excellent, it is difficult for some Dutch oven users to produce visually appealing meat from the steamy oven.

The trick is simple

Irrespective of the spices and flavors you use on any meat or poultry, brown the meat first. Add enough butter, bacon, or fat in the hot oven to brown the meat to make a good oil cover on the bottom, heat the oven, then place the meat in the oven and sear or brown well.

This will lock in natural juices and make the texture and color typical of grilled or fried meats. Once the meat has browned well on all sides, remove any residual fat droppings, add seasonings you want, put on the lid and cook for 30-35 minutes for 1 pound of beef or lamb, and 25-30 minutes for 1 pound of poultry.

Vegetables

Fresh garden vegetables are a wonderful accompaniment to any Dutch oven meal. Many vegetables prepared in a Dutch oven are cooked in a sauce. Still, they can also be steamed or cooked on a conventional stovetop.

However, choose to roast or bake vegetables in a Dutch oven. They will take approximately 3 minutes per inch of the oven's diameter to cook.

Using a 10-inch oven will take approximately 30-36 minutes to cook a squash-filled 10-inch oven. Sauces can cook vegetables, such as new peas and potatoes in white sauce, broccoli in cheese sauce, or sour cream potatoes. They should be brought to a rapid boil, the water discarded, sauces added, and then boiled simultaneously as the other vegetables in the same pot.

PART 2:
THE RECIPES

CHAPTER 4:
BREAKFAST RECIPES

AWESOME PANCAKE

Servings: 4-5
Cooking Time: 20 minutes
Coal Quantity And Placement: 20 Coals (10 Underneath/ 10 Above)

Ingredients

* 3 large eggs
* ½ cup flour
* ½ cup milk
* 1 tablespoon sugar
* 1 pinch cinnamon
* 4 tablespoons butter

Method

1. Make a campfire by arranging a bed of coals and allowing the fire to burn until the coals are red hot about 10 coals.
2. Place the Dutch oven on top of the coals.
3. In a large mixing bowl, combine the eggs, milk, sugar, and cinnamon and stir well.
4. Blend the batter until it is smooth.
5. Place the butter in the Dutch oven and allow it to melt.
6. Place the lid on the pan and pour in the batter.
7. 10 hot coals should be placed on top.
8. 20 minutes in the oven
9. Cut the pancake into wedges after removing it from the pan.
10. Serve with syrup and enjoy!

Nutritional Values (Per Serving)

Calories: 227; Fat: 10 g; Carbohydrates: 28 g; Protein: 6 g

THE GREAT STRAWBERRY DUTCH

Servings: 6
Cooking Time: 25 minutes
Coal Quantity And Placement: 28 Coals (12 Underneath/ 16 Above)

Ingredients

* 3 large eggs
* 2/3 cup all-purpose flour
* 2/3 cup milk
* 3/8 teaspoon salt
* ¼ cup unsalted butter, cut into pieces
* 1-pint strawberries halved
* 1/3 cup sugar

Method

1. Build a campfire by arranging a bed of coal and letting the fire burn until coals are red hot, 12 coals on bottom
2. Place Dutch Oven over the fire
3. Take a bowl and whisk in eggs until frothy, add flour, milk, salt, and whisk well
4. Melt in butter to Oven and let it melt, add batter to over and place the lid
5. Place 16 coals on top and bake for 20 minutes
6. Once the batter puffs up
7. While the pancake is baking, take a small bowl and add strawberries, sugar and stir well
8. Pour strawberry mixture over middle of Dutch baby, cut into wedges and serve
9. Enjoy!

For stovetop cooking, the required temperature (approximately) is 425 Degrees F/220 Degrees C For a 10-inch Dutch Oven

Nutritional Values (Per Serving)

Calories: 150; Fat: 3.5g; Carbohydrates: 27 g; Protein: 2 g

BROWN SUGAR OATMEAL

Servings: 8
Cooking Time: 30 minutes
Coal Quantity And Placement: 26 Coals (11 Underneath/ 15 Above)

Ingredients

* Cooking oil as needed
* 4 cups old fashioned rolled oats
* ½ cup brown sugar
* 2 teaspoons baking powder
* ½ teaspoon salt
* 2 large eggs, lightly beaten
* 3 cups of milk

Method

1. Build a campfire by laying a coal bed on the ground and burning until the coals are red hot, with 11 coals on the bottom.
2. Heat up your Dutch Oven over coals, then add the oats, brown sugar, baking powder, and salt.
3. Combine the eggs and milk in a mixing bowl.
4. Place 15 coals on top of the pot and cover it with a lid.
5. Preheat oven to 350°F and bake for 30 minutes, or until mixture is firm.
6. Slicing into wedges
7. Serve and have fun!

For stovetop cooking, the required temperature (approximately) is 400 Degrees F/205 Degrees C For a 10-inch Dutch Oven

Nutritional Values (Per Serving)

Calories: 260; Fat: 5 g; Carbohydrates: 47 g; Protein: 5 g

PERFECT STEEL CUTS

Servings: 6
Cooking Time: 25 minutes
Coal Quantity And Placement: 14 Coals (14 Underneath/ 0 Above)

Ingredients

* 1 and ½ cups steel cut oats
* 5 cups of water
* ¼ cup strawberry preserves
* Pinch of salt
* 3 tablespoons brown sugar

Method

1. Build a campfire by arranging a bed of coal and letting the fire burn until coals are red hot, 14 coals on bottom
2. Place Dutch Oven over hot coals and add oats, toast for about 3 minutes until golden
3. Stir in water, preserves, salt and bring to a boil
4. Remove 4-6 coals from beneath and lower heat until it comes to a simmer
5. Add more water if needed and cook for 20 minutes until tender
6. Serve with a sprinkle of brown sugar/maple syrup
7. Enjoy!

For stovetop cooking, the required temperature (approximately) is 250 Degrees F/120 Degrees C For a 10-inch Dutch Oven

Nutritional Values (Per Serving)

Calories: 560; Fat: 15 g; Carbohydrates: 96 g; Protein: 14 g

THE ALL AMERICAN BREAKFAST

Servings: 4-5
Cooking Time: 90 minutes
Coal Quantity And Placement: 18 Coals (6 Underneath/ 12 Above)

Ingredients

* 1-pound/ 0.5 kg mild pork sausage
* 1 large onion, chopped
* 1 garlic clove, minced
* 1 red bell pepper, diced
* 1 green pepper, chopped
* 1-2 pounds/ 0.5-1 kg, frozen hash brown potatoes, shredded
* 12 large eggs, beaten
* 16 ounces/450 grams cheddar cheese, shredded

Method

1. Build a campfire by laying a coal bed on the ground and burning it until the coals are red hot, with 6 coals underneath.
2. Heat the Dutch oven cast iron over high heat, then add the sausage, onion, and garlic and cook until the sausage is tender and the onions are translucent.
3. Cook for 15 minutes with red bell pepper, green bell pepper, and hash brown potatoes.
4. Pour the eggs evenly over the potatoes and allow them to sink.
5. Place 6 coals underneath the Dutch Oven and 12 coals on top.
6. Bake the eggs for 40 minutes, then top with cheddar cheese.
7. Cover
8. Cook for another 5 minutes.
9. Serve and have fun!

For stovetop cooking, the required temperature (approximately) is 325 Degrees F/160 Degrees C For a 10-inch Dutch Oven

Nutritional Values (Per Serving)

Calories: 970; Fat: 7 g; Carbohydrates: 21 g; Protein: 48 g

HONEY AND ALMOND GRANOLA BARS

Servings: 12
Cooking Time: 5 minutes
Coal Quantity And Placement: 10 Coals (10 Underneath/ 0 Above)

Ingredients

* * Cooking oil
* * 2 and ½ cups old-fashioned rolled oats
* * ½ cup almond, chopped
* * ½ cup honey
* * ¼ cup unsalted butter, cut into pieces
* * ¼ cup brown sugar
* * ¼ teaspoon kosher salt

Method

1. Build a campfire by arranging a bed of coal and letting the fire burn until coals are red hot, 10 coals on bottom
2. Place Dutch Oven over a bed of coals
3. Add oats, almond and stir cook until golden brown; it should take about 3 minutes
4. Transfer oats and almond to bowl
5. Add honey, butter, brown sugar, and salt to Dutch Oven
6. Cook until the butter and sugar melts
7. Stir in oats, almonds into butter and mix well
8. Let it cool
9. Cut into bars and serve
10. Enjoy!

For stovetop cooking, the required temperature (approximately) is 200 Degrees F /100 Degrees C For a 10-inch Dutch Oven

Nutritional Values (Per Serving)

Calories: 200; Fat: 8 g; Carbohydrates: 29 g; Protein: 4 g

HASH BROWNS

Servings: 8
Cooking Time: 30 minutes
Coal Quantity And Placement: 21 Coals (7 Underneath/ 14 Above)

Ingredients

* 2 potatoes, shredded
* 6 whole eggs
* 1 onion, diced
* 1 tablespoon avocado oil
* 3 ounces/90 grams bacon, chopped
* ½ teaspoon chili flakes
* ½ teaspoon salt
* 1 teaspoon ground black pepper

Method

1. Build a campfire by laying a bed of coals on the ground and allowing the fire to burn until the coals are red hot, about 7 coals on the bottom.
2. Fill your Dutch oven with shredded potato and diced onion.
3. Stir in the avocado oil and chopped bacon.
4. Stir in the chili flakes and salt, as well as the ground black pepper.
5. Whisk in the eggs thoroughly.
6. Pour the eggs over the potatoes and stir to combine.
7. Cook for 30 minutes with the lid on and 14 hot coals on top.
8. Serve and have fun!

For stovetop cooking, the required temperature (approximately) is 350 Degrees F/175 Degrees C For a 10-inch Dutch Oven

Nutritional Values (Per Serving)

Calories: 210; Fat: 12 g; Carbohydrates: 26 g; Protein: 2 g

SPINACH AND CHEESE LASAGNA

Servings: 6-8
Cooking Time: 60 minutes
Coal Quantity And Placement: 28 Coals (8 Underneath/ 20 Above)

Ingredients

* 1 tablespoon olive oil
* 24 ounces/680 grams of pasta sauce
* 16 ounces/452 grams no-boil lasagna noodles
* 3 cups fresh baby spinach
* 2 cups Italian Style cheese blend, shredded
* 1 tablespoon dried Italian seasoning blend

Method

1. Build a campfire by arranging a bed of coal and letting the fire burn until coals are red hot, 8 coals on bottom
2. Take your Dutch Oven and spread oil on the bottom, spread ½ cup sauce on the bottom
3. Create a layer of noodles, arrange, so they don't overlap. Top with ½ cup sauce, 1 cup spinach, ½ cup cheese
4. Add two more layers, repeating the process. Finish with noodle layer, remaining sauce, and ½ cup cheese
5. Sprinkle Italian seasoning
6. Place Dutch Oven over a bed of coals, put the lid on, and place 20 coals on top
7. Bake for 50-60 minutes until noodles become tender and cheese melts
8. Serve and enjoy!

For stovetop cooking, the required temperature (approximately) is 450 Degrees F/240 Degrees C For a 10-inch Dutch Oven

Nutritional Values (Per Serving)

Calories: 1180; Fat: 66 g; Carbohydrates: 84 g; Protein: 62 g

QUINOA WITH SHREDDED BEEF PICO DE GALLO

Servings: 6-8
Cooking Time: 2-3 Hours

Ingredients

*   2 cups cooked quinoa
*   2 pounds medium roasted beef
*   3-4 slices bacon
*   1 cup cheese, shredded
*   1 large tomato, chopped
*   1 large onion, chopped
*   1 large russet potato, cubed
*   1 turnip, cubed

*   ½ small green bell pepper
*   ½ Anaheim pepper
*   1 teaspoon ginger, minced
*   ¼ jalapeno pepper
*   Cilantro, chopped
*   1 tablespoon garlic, chopped
*   ¾ cup red wine vinegar
*   1 teaspoon cumin
*   ½ teaspoon chili powder

Method

1. Cut your beef into 1-2 inch cubes
2. Transfer them to your Dutch Oven
3. Add 2/3 of onion around beef and arrange bacon slices on top of onions
4. Add minced ginger, red wine vinegar, chopped garlic, cumin, chili powder
5. Season with salt and pepper according to your taste
6. Cook on medium for about 1-2 hours until the beef is tender, add potato and turnip once the beef is almost tender
7. Once tender, remove beef from Dutch Oven and shred it well
8. Remove potato/turnip mixture and leave the liquid
9. Add cooked quinoa to the bottom of your Dutch Oven and spread it evenly
10. Layer potato/turnip mixture on top of quinoa
11. Add shredded beef
12. Sprinkle shredded cheese
13. Make the pico de gallo by adding chopped tomato, pepper, and onion to a bowl and seasoning t with salt and pepper
14. Carefully place pico de gallo in the center of your dish and garnish with cilantro
15. Enjoy!

Nutritional Values (Per Serving)

Calories: 1070; Fat: 42 g; Carbohydrates: 66 g; Protein: 5 g

CHAPTER 5:
CHILIES, SOUPS AND STEWS RECIPES

DELICIOUS THAI CURRY

Servings: 6
Cooking Time: 15 minutes
Coal Quantity And Placement: 15 Coals (15 Underneath/ 0 Above)

Ingredients

* 3 tablespoons cooking oil
* 1-3 tablespoons Thai Red Curry Paste
* 6 cups vegetable broth
* 45 ounces/1275 grams pumpkin puree
* 28 ounces/800 grams of coconut milk
* Salt as needed
* ¼ cup cilantro, chopped

Method

1. Build a campfire by laying a bed of coals on the ground and allowing the fire to burn until the coals are red hot, about 15 coals on the bottom. Place the Dutch Oven over the coals, add the oil, and allow it to heat up.
2. Allow the oil to simmer before adding the curry paste and cooking for 1 minute.
3. Bring to a boil with the broth and pumpkin puree, stirring constantly.
4. Bring to a boil with coconut milk.
5. Cook for 10 minutes, then reduce the heat by removing the coals if necessary.
6. Season with salt and cilantro, and serve immediately.
7. Enjoy!

For stovetop cooking, the required temperature (approximately) is 275 Degrees F/135 Degrees C For a 10-inch Dutch Oven

Nutritional Values (Per Serving)

Calories: 288; Fat: 10 g; Carbohydrates: 24 g; Protein: 27 g

ITALIAN TOMATO AND ORZO SOUP

Servings: 6
Cooking Time: 25 minutes
Coal Quantity And Placement: 15 Coals (15 Underneath/ 0 Above)

Ingredients

* 2 tablespoons olive oil
* 1 onion, diced
* 8 cups vegetable broth
* 28 ounces/ 800 grams Italian Styled, diced tomatoes
* 1 teaspoon salt
* 1.2 teaspoon ground black pepper
* 2 cups orzo pasta
* 4 cups spinach

Method

1. Build a campfire by laying a bed of coals on the ground and allowing it to burn until the coals are red hot (15 coals on the bottom). Place the Dutch Oven over the coals, add the oil, and allow it to heat up.
2. Cook for 5 minutes or until onion is tender.
3. Bring the broth, tomatoes, salt, and pepper to a boil.
4. Cook for approximately 10-15 minutes.
5. Cook for 5-6 minutes after adding the pasta.
6. Cook for another 2 minutes after adding the spinach.
7. Serve and have fun!

For stovetop cooking, the required temperature (approximately) is 275 Degrees F/135 Degrees C For a 10-inch Dutch Oven

Nutritional Values (Per Serving)

Calories: 247; Fat: 12 g; Carbohydrates: 23 g; Protein: 11 g

GREEN AND BREAD SOUP

Servings: 6
Cooking Time: 35 minutes
Coal Quantity And Placement: 12 Coals (12 Underneath/ 0 Above)

Ingredients

* 2 tablespoons olive oil
* 1 onion, diced 10-12 green kale leaves
* 1 teaspoon salt
* ½ teaspoon ground black pepper
* 14 ounces/ 400 grams cannellini beans
* 4 cups vegetable broth
* 2 cups stale French bread, crusts removed

Method

1. Build a campfire by arranging a bed of coal and letting the fire burn until coals are red hot, 12 coals on bottom
2. Place Dutch Oven over hot coal bed and add olive oil, let it heat up
3. Add onion and cook for 5 minutes
4. Add greens, salt, pepper, cook until wilt
5. Add ¼ cup water if needed
6. Add beans, broth, bring to simmer
7. Stir in bread, cover pot
8. Remove a few coals from the bottom and let it simmer for 30 minutes and the bread completely dissolves into the soup
9. Serve and enjoy!

For stovetop cooking, the required temperature (approximately) is 200 Degrees F/95 Degrees C For a 10-inch Dutch Oven

Nutritional Values (Per Serving)

Calories: 265; Fat: 3 g; Carbohydrates: 49 g; Protein: 9 g

BUTTERNUT SQUASH AND WHITE BEAN STEW

Servings: 8
Cooking Time: 40 minutes
Coal Quantity And Placement: 12 Coals (12 Underneath/ 0 Above)

Ingredients

* 2 tablespoons olive oil
* 1 onion, diced
* 2 garlic cloves, minced
* 4 cups butternut squash, cubed and peeled
* 14 ounces/ 400 grams tomatoes, diced
* 1 teaspoon salt
* ½ teaspoon ground black pepper
* 2 cups of water
* 15 ounces/425 grams cannellini beans, drained and rinsed

Method

1. Build a campfire by arranging a bed of coal and letting the fire burn until coals are red hot, 12 coals on bottom
2. Place Dutch Oven over a bed of coals, let it heat up
3. Add onion, cook for 5 minutes
4. Stir in garlic, squash, tomatoes, salt, pepper,
5. Add water, bring to simmer
6. Remove 2-3 coals from underneath pot
7. Let it simmer for 25 minutes
8. Stir in beans, continue to simmer for 10 minutes
9. Serve and enjoy!

For stovetop cooking, the required temperature (approximately) is 200 Degrees F/95 Degrees C For a 10-inch Dutch Oven

Nutritional Values (Per Serving)

Calories: 90; Fat: 1 g; Carbohydrates: 20 g; Protein: 1 g

CORN CHOWDER AND GREEN CHILE

Servings: 4
Cooking Time: 20 minutes
Coal Quantity And Placement: 10 Coals (10 Underneath/ 0 Above)

Ingredients

* 1 tablespoon olive oil
* 1 onion, chopped
* 16 ounces/ 450 grams frozen corn, thawed
* 2 cups whole milk, divided
* 14 ounces/ 400 grams fire-roasted green chiles, diced
* ¾ teaspoon salt
* 1 cup sharp cheddar cheese, divided

Method

1. Build a campfire by laying a bed of coals on the ground and allowing the fire to burn until the coals are red hot, about 10 coals on the bottom.
2. Place the Dutch oven over a bed of coals and heat it up.
3. Cook for 5 minutes after adding the onion.
4. Cook for another 3 minutes after adding the corn.
5. Bring the milk, chiles, and salt to a simmer, remove some coals if necessary and let it simmer for 10 minutes.
6. Stir in half of the cheese until it has melted.
7. Serve immediately with the remaining cheese as a garnish.
8. Enjoy!

For stovetop cooking, the required temperature (approximately) is 200 Degrees F /95 Degrees C For a 10-inch Dutch Oven

Nutritional Values (Per Serving)

Calories: 280; Fat: 18 g; Carbohydrates: 29 g; Protein: 8 g

CREAMY SALMON CHOWDER

Servings: 4
Cooking Time: 20 minutes
Coal Quantity And Placement: 12 Coals (12 Underneath/ 0 Above)

Ingredients

* ½ pound/0.25 kg bacon, sliced
* ½ pound/ 0.25 kg red potatoes, diced
* 1 cup of water
* 3 cups half and half
* 12 ounces/ 340 grams salmon fillets
* ½ teaspoon salt
* ¼ teaspoon ground black pepper
* 2 teaspoons lemon, freshly squeezed

Method

1. Build a campfire by arranging a bed of coal and letting the fire burn until coals are red hot, 12 coals on bottom
2. Place Dutch Oven over a bed of coals
3. Add bacon, cook for 5 minutes until slightly browned and fat has been rendered
4. Transfer bacon to a paper-lined plate
5. Add potatoes to bacon fat, cook for 5 minutes until browned
6. Add water, cook for 12 minutes
7. Stir in half and half, salmon, salt, pepper, and bring to a simmer
8. Remove 2 coals from underneath, cook for 5 minutes more
9. Remove pan from heat
10. Stir in lemon juice
11. Serve hot and enjoy!

For stovetop cooking, the required temperature (approximately) is 225 Degrees F /110 Degrees C For a 10-inch Dutch Oven

Nutritional Values (Per Serving)

Calories: 220; Fat: 13 g; Carbohydrates: 22 g; Protein: 4 g

POTATO STEW AND CHICKPEA SOUP

Servings: 6
Cooking Time: 25 minutes
Coal Quantity And Placement: 10 Coals (10 Underneath/ 0 Above)

Ingredients

* 2 tablespoons cooking oil
* 3 shallots, diced
* 1 tablespoon fresh ginger, grated
* 2 cups potatoes, diced
* 2 tablespoons curry powder
* 1 teaspoon salt
* ½ teaspoon fresh ground black pepper
* 30 ounces/850 grams chickpeas, drained and rinsed
* 3 cups of water

Method

1. Build a campfire by arranging a bed of coal and letting the fire burn until coals are red hot, 10 coals on bottom
2. Place Dutch Oven over hot coals, let it heat up
3. Add shallots, cook for 5 minutes
4. Stir in ginger, cook for 1 minute
5. Stir in potatoes, curry powder, salt, pepper and cook for 2 minutes
6. Add chickpeas, water and bring to a simmer
7. Remove 2 coals from underneath, let it simmer for 15 minutes
8. Once the potatoes are tender, and the sauce is thick
9. Serve and enjoy!

For stovetop cooking, the required temperature (approximately) is 200 Degrees F/95 Degrees C For a 10-inch Dutch Oven

Nutritional Values (Per Serving)

Calories: 190; Fat: 9 g; Carbohydrates: 20 g; Protein: 4 g

CHAPTER 6:
MAINS RECIPES

BAKED EGGPLANT PARMESAN

Servings: 4
Cooking Time: 35 minutes
Coal Quantity And Placement: 24 Coals (Follow instructions for placement)

Ingredients

* 1 large eggplant, peeled and cut into ½ inch thick slices
* 1 teaspoon salt
* 2 large eggs, salt
* 1 and ½ cups seasoned dry bread crumbs
* ¼ cup olive oil
* 3 cups marinara sauce
* 12 ounces/340 grams shredded Italian cheese mix

Method

1. Build a campfire by arranging a bed of coal and letting the fire burn until coals are red hot, 12 coals on bottom
2. Arrange eggplant slices in a single layer on paper towels, sprinkle both sides with salt
3. Let them sit for 30 minutes
4. Wipe salt and pat them dry
5. Place eggs in I shallow bowl, place breadcrumbs in a separate shallow bowl, dip the eggplant into eggs, and then into bread crumbs
6. Place Dutch Oven over coals, add oil and let it heat up
7. Add slices and brown for 2 minutes per side, until browned
8. Transfer to browned eggplant slices to a paper towel
9. Remove oven from heat, arrange half of the browned slices in the bottom of the pot, add ½ of marinara sauce,
10. Sprinkle half of the cheese, repeat by creating more layers of eggplant, sauce, and cheese
11. Place Oven over 8 hot coals, place 16 on top of the lid
12. Bake for 25 minutes until bubbly
13. Serve and enjoy!

For stovetop cooking, the required temperature (approximately) is 375 Degrees F/190 Degrees C For a 10-inch Dutch Oven

Nutritional Values (Per Serving)

Calories: 600; Fat: 30 g; Carbohydrates: 67 g; Protein: 18 g

AWESOME BROCCOLI AND CHICKPEA CURRY

Servings: 6-8
Cooking Time: 15 minutes
Coal Quantity And Placement: 12 Coals (12 Underneath/ 0 Above)

Ingredients

* 2 tablespoons cooking oil
* 2 garlic cloves, minced
* ¼ cup Thai red curry paste
* 2 heads broccoli, cut into florets
* 15 ounces/425 grams of coconut milk
* 14 ounces/396 grams chickpeas, drained and rinsed
* 1 tablespoon cornstarch, dissolved in 1/4 cup cold water

Method

1. Build a campfire by arranging a bed of coal and letting the fire burn until coals are red hot, 12 coals on bottom
2. Place Dutch Oven over hot coal, add garlic, and cook for 3 minutes
3. Stir in curry paste, cook for 1 minute
4. Add broccoli and cook for 2-3 minutes
5. Add coconut milk, cook for 3 minutes
6. Add chickpeas, bring back to boil
7. Stir in cornstarch mixture and cook well for 2 minutes more
8. Once the sauce is thick, serve and enjoy!

*For stovetop cooking, the required temperature (approximately) is 325 Degrees F /160 Degrees C For a 10-inch Dutch Oven

Nutritional Values (Per Serving)

Calories: 300; Fat: 20 g; Carbohydrates: 21 g; Protein: 12 g

GOLDEN MAC AND CHEESE

Servings: 6-8
Cooking Time: 10 minutes
Coal Quantity And Placement: 8 Coals (8 Underneath/ 0 Above)

Ingredients

* ½ cup unsalted butter
* 2 large eggs
* 12 ounces/340 grams evaporated milk
* 2 teaspoon salt
* 1 teaspoon fresh ground black pepper
* 1 and ½ pounds/0.5 kg cheese, shredded
* 16 ounces/452 grams macaroni, cooked

Method

1. Build a campfire by arranging a bed of coal and letting the fire burn until coals are red hot, 8 coals on bottom
2. Take your Dutch Oven and place it over hot coals, add butter and let it melt
3. Take a bowl and whisk in eggs, milk, salt, pepper; whisk the egg mixture into melted butter
4. Add cheese and pasta, cook for 3 minutes until sauce is thick and creamy
5. Serve and enjoy!

For stovetop cooking, the required temperature (approximately) is 300 Degrees F/140 Degrees C For a 10-inch Dutch Oven

Nutritional Values (Per Serving)

Calories: 210; Fat: 12 g; Carbohydrates: 20 g; Protein: 7 g

MAJESTIC COCONUT THAI CURRY CHICKEN

Servings: 4-6
Cooking Time: 25 minutes
Coal Quantity And Placement: 12 Coals (12 Underneath/ 0 Above)

Ingredients

* 2 tablespoons cooking oil
* 1 onion, diced
* 1-3 tablespoons Thai Red Curry Paste
* 14 ounces/ 400 grams of coconut milk
* 2 cups of water
* 1 tablespoon brown sugar
* 1 and ½ pounds/0.6 kg boneless, skinless chicken thighs
* Salt and pepper to taste

Method

1. Build a campfire by laying a bed of coals on the ground and allowing it to burn until the coals are red hot, with 12 coals on the bottom. Place the Dutch Oven over the hot coals and allow it to heat up.
2. Cook for 5 minutes or until the onion is soft.
3. Cook for 1-2 minutes after adding the curry paste.
4. Bring coconut milk, water, brown sugar, chicken, salt, and pepper to a boil.
5. Remove 4 coals from underneath and reduce to low heat, continuing to cook for another 15 minutes or until they are tender. Serve hot and enjoy!

For stovetop cooking, the required temperature (approximately) is 225 Degrees F/107 Degrees C For a 10-inch Dutch Oven

Nutritional Values (Per Serving)

Calories: 210; Fat: 13 g; Carbohydrates: 17 g; Protein: 5 g

SPICED UP CHICKEN CUBES

Servings: 4
Cooking Time: 20 minutes
Coal Quantity And Placement: 23 Coals (7 Underneath/ 16 Above)

Ingredients

* 11 ounces/ 312 grams chicken fillet
* 1 tablespoon paprika
* 2 tablespoons olive oil
* ½ teaspoon salt
* 1-ounce/ 28 grams basil

Method

1. Build a campfire by laying a bed of coals on the ground and allowing the fire to burn until the coals are red hot, about 7 coals on the bottom.
2. Cut the chicken fillet into cubes and season with paprika, olive oil, salt, and basil.
3. Stir the meat in the Dutch Oven thoroughly.
4. Place the Dutch Oven over a bed of hot coals.
5. Place a lid on top and 16 hot coals on top of that.
6. Cooking time: 20 minutes
7. Serve and have fun!

For stovetop cooking, the required temperature (approximately) is 375 Degrees F/190 Degrees C For a 10-inch Dutch Oven

Nutritional Values (Per Serving)

Calories: 850; Fat: 45 g; Carbohydrates: 74 g; Protein: 35 g

SPICY CHICKEN SAUSAGES

Servings: 4
Cooking Time: 30 minutes
Coal Quantity And Placement: 21 Coals (7 Underneath/ 14 Above)

Ingredients

* 13 ounces/ 368 grams chicken, ground
* 1 tablespoon paprika
* ½ teaspoon salt
* 1 teaspoon ground pepper
* 1 tablespoon olive oil
* 1 teaspoon dried dill
* 1 teaspoon dried parsley
* ½ teaspoon chili flakes

Method

1. Build a campfire by arranging a bed of coal and letting the fire burn until coals are red hot, 7 coals on bottom
2. Take a bowl and mix in ground chicken, paprika, salt, ground black pepper, dried dill, dried parsley, chili flakes
3. Stir well
4. Make medium-sized sausages
5. Place your Dutch Oven over coals and let it heat up for 5 minutes
6. Add oil and let it heat up
7. Add sausages and cover with the lid, place 14 coals on top and cook for 30 minutes
8. Serve and enjoy!

For stovetop cooking, the required temperature (approximately) is 350 Degrees F/175 Degrees C For a 10-inch Dutch Oven

Nutritional Values (Per Serving)

Calories: 94; Fat: 6 g; Carbohydrates: 0 g; Protein: 9 g

SPICY CHIPOTLE ROAST PORK

Servings: 8
Cooking Time: 70 minutes
Coal Quantity And Placement: 25 Coals (12 Underneath/ 17 by Above, replacing some from the bottom as needed)

Ingredients

* 1 cup freshly orange, freshly squeezed
* ½ cup lime juice, freshly squeezed
* 1 chipotle chile, adobo + 2 tablespoons of sauce from a jar
* 2 garlic cloves, minced
* Salt and pepper to taste
* 2 pounds / 1kg boneless pork roast
* 2 tablespoons cooking oil

Method

1. Build a campfire by laying a coal bed on the ground and burning until the coals are red hot, with 12 coals on the bottom.
2. Add orange juice, lime juice, chipotle chile, adobo sauce, garlic, salt, and pepper to a large mixing bowl.
3. Add the pork, turn to coat well, and set aside for 60 minutes to marinate.
4. 30 minutes before cooking, remove from bag.
5. Place the Dutch Oven over the coals to heat up.
6. Remove the roast from the marinade and set aside any excess liquid. Cook for 10 minutes to ensure even browning on all sides.
7. Remove 4 coals from underneath the pot, place 17 coals on top of the lid, then add the reserved marinade.
8. Cook for another 30 minutes, checking for doneness as needed.
9. Remove some coals after 30 minutes and keep it on low heat for 15-30 minutes, or until the pork is done.
10. Remove the roast from the oven and cover it with foil. Allow for a 10-minute rest before slicing.
11. Carve the roast into 14 inch thick slices and serve with a thick marinade that has simmered and thickened in the pot.
12. Enjoy!

For stovetop cooking, the required temperature (approximately) is 400 Degrees F/205 Degrees C For a 10-inch Dutch Oven

Nutritional Values (Per Serving)

Calories: 230; Fat: 6 g; Carbohydrates: 32 g; Protein: 11 g

CIDER AND DIJON PORK ROAST

Servings: 6
Cooking Time: 40 minutes
Coal Quantity And Placement: 25 Coals (12 Underneath/ 18 Above, taking 5 coals from bottom)

Ingredients

* 3 tablespoons olive oil, divided
* 2 pork tenderloins, 2 and ½ pounds/ 1.2 kg, each cut into 2 pieces
* Salt and pepper as needed
* 1 large onion, chopped
* ½ cup dry white wine
* 1 tablespoon Dijon mustard
* 1 cup apple cider

Method

1. Build a campfire by arranging a bed of coal and letting the fire burn until coals are red hot, 12 coals on bottom
2. Season pork generously with salt and pepper
3. Place Dutch Ove over hot coals, let it heat up
4. Add pork and sear until all sides are browned, should take about 8 minutes
5. Transfer to plate
6. Add onion to pot, cook for 5 minutes
7. Add wine to the pot, stirring, and cook for 3 minutes
8. Return pork to pot alongside any juices, spread mustard over pork, and pour cider over top
9. Cover pot, remove 5 coals from the bottom, and place 18 coals on top
10. Cook for 25 minutes until pork is cooked through
11. Let it rest for 10 minutes, carve into ¼ inch thick slices and serve with onions, pour the sauce over top

For stovetop cooking, the required temperature (approximately) is 400 Degrees F/205 Degrees C For a 10-inch Dutch Oven

Nutritional Values (Per Serving)

Calories: 849; Fat: 53 g; Carbohydrates: 40 g; Protein: 50 g

BAKED TORTELLINI SAUSAGE

Servings: 4
Cooking Time: 25 minutes
Coal Quantity And Placement: 23 Coals (8 Underneath/ 17 Above)

Ingredients

* 2 cups of water
* 9 ounces/260 grams fresh cheese tortellini
* 2 tablespoons extra virgin olive oil
* 1-pound/ 0.5kg Italian Pork sausage, cut into small pieces
* 15 ounces/425 grams marinara sauce
* Salt and pepper to taste
* 1 cup mozzarella cheese, shredded
* 1 cup Italian breadcrumbs

Method

1. Build a campfire by placing a bed of coals on the bottom of the fire and allowing it to burn until the coals are red hot.
2. Fill your Dutch Oven with water and place it over coals to bring it to a boil.
3. Cook for 5 minutes with the cheese tortellini, drain and set aside.
4. Heat the oil in your Dutch Oven, then add the sausage and cook for 5 minutes.
5. Season with salt and pepper and add the cooked tortellini and marinara sauce.
6. Cook for another 5 minutes.
7. Stir in the mozzarella cheese until everything is well combined.
8. Toss in some breadcrumbs.
9. Cover with a lid and 17 coals, and bake for 10 minutes, or until golden.
10. Serve and have fun!

For stovetop cooking, the required temperature (approximately) is 375 Degrees F/190 Degrees C For a 10-inch Dutch Oven

Nutritional Values (Per Serving)

Calories: 170; Fat: 7 g; Carbohydrates: 0 g; Protein: 12 g

LOVELY CASSOULET

Servings: 4
Cooking Time: 30 minutes
Coal Quantity And Placement: 25 Coals (8 Underneath/ 17 Above)

Ingredients

* 5 slices bacon, cut into ½ inch thick slices
* 1 medium yellow onion, chopped
* 2 garlic cloves, minced
* 1 cup chicken broth
* 14 and ½ ounces/412 grams crushed tomatoes
* 28 ounces/800 grams cannellini beans, rinsed and drained
* 2 cups fresh bread crumbs
* 3 tablespoons butter, melted
* ¼ cup fresh parsley, chopped

Method

1. Build a campfire by arranging a bed of coal and letting the fire burn until coals are red hot, 8 coals on bottom
2. Take your Dutch Oven and place it over coals, let it heat up
3. Add bacon and cook until brown
4. Remove with a slotted spoon and transfer plate, leaving the fat behind
5. Add onions, Sauté for a few minutes until soft, add garlic and Sauté for 2 minutes
6. Add broth, tomatoes, beans, bacon, and stir
7. Transfer to Dutch Oven and cook for 15 minutes
8. Take a medium bowl and add bread crumbs, melted butter, parsley
9. Place lid on top and add 17 coals on top, let it bake for 10 minutes until top is golden brown
10. Serve and enjoy!

For stovetop cooking, the required temperature (approximately) is 400 Degrees F/205 Degrees C For a 10-inch Dutch Oven

Nutritional Values (Per Serving)

Calories: 240; Fat: 12 g; Carbohydrates: 17 g; Protein: 14 g

CLASSIC PORK CHILI

Servings: 4
Cooking Time: 40 minutes
Coal Quantity And Placement: 21 Coals (7 Underneath/ 14 Above)

Ingredients

* 7 ounces/200 grams pork, ground
* 1 cup red beans, canned
* 1 sweet pepper, chopped
* 1 tomato, chopped
* 2 tablespoons tomato paste
* ¼ cup sweet corn
* 1 onion, chopped
* 1 cup chicken stock
* 1 teaspoon salt
* 1 teaspoon ground black pepper
* ½ teaspoon chili pepper
* 1 jalapeno pepper
* 1 tablespoon olive oil
* 1 teaspoon dried oregano

Method

1. Build a campfire by arranging a bed of coal and letting the fire burn until coals are red hot, with 7 coals on the bottom.
2. Place Dutch Oven over hot coals and let it heat up for 5 minutes
3. Add ground pork, chopped tomato, tomato paste, sweet corn, onion, salt, ground black pepper, olive oil, dried oregano to Oven
4. Sir in remaining ingredients and cook for 10 minutes
5. Add chopped chili pepper and jalapeno
6. Add sweet pepper and red beans
7. Stir in the mix, add chicken stock
8. Stir well and place the lid
9. Place 14 coals above the lid and cook for 30 minutes
10. Once done, serve and enjoy!

For stovetop cooking, the required temperature (approximately) is 350 Degrees F/175 Degrees C For a 10-inch Dutch Oven

Nutritional Values (Per Serving)

Calories: 340; Fat: 12 g; Carbohydrates: 35 g; Protein: 23 g

BEEF UP GARLIC POT ROAST

Servings: 6-8
Cooking Time: 85 minutes
Coal Quantity And Placement: 24 Coals (10 Underneath/ 17 Above, take 3 from the bottom when needed)

Ingredients

* 2 tablespoons olive oil
* 1 (3 pounds)/1.2 kg boneless beef chuck roast
* Salt and pepper to taste
* 1 cup dry red wine
* 1 cup beef broth
* 4 carrots, peeled and cut into 2-inch pieces
* 8 garlic cloves, smashed

Method

1. Build a campfire by laying a bed of coals on the ground and allowing the fire to burn until the coals are red hot, about 10 coals on the bottom.
2. Dutch had been positioned. Heat the oven over coals and add the oil.
3. Rub olive oil all over the roast and season with salt and pepper to taste.
4. Cook for 10 minutes, turning the roast to brown on all sides.
5. Place the roast in the pot with the wine, broth, carrots, and garlic.
6. Remove 3 coals from the bottom of the pot and replace them with 17 coals on top.
7. Cook for 75 minutes or until the roast is tender. Remove the roast from the pot and set it aside for 10 minutes.
8. Slice and serve with carrots and vegetable juices.
9. Serve and have fun!

For stovetop cooking, the required temperature (approximately) is 375 Degrees F/190 Degrees C For a 10-inch Dutch Oven

Nutritional Values (Per Serving)

Calories: 611; Fat: 35 g; Carbohydrates: 43 g; Protein: 31 g

BUTTER AND GARLIC BAKED SHRIMP

Servings: 4
Cooking Time: 15 minutes
Coal Quantity And Placement: 16 Coals (10 Underneath/ 24 Above)

Ingredients

* ¼ cup unsalted butter
* 2 and ½ pounds/ 1.2 kg shrimp, peeled and deveined
* 6 garlic cloves, minced
* Juice of 1 large lemon
* ¾ cup white wine
* 1 cup tomatoes, chopped
* ½ teaspoon salt
* ½ teaspoon fresh ground black pepper

Method

1. Build a campfire by arranging a bed of coal and letting the fire burn until coals are red hot, 6 coals on bottom
2. Place Dutch Oven over coals, add butter and let it melt
3. Add shrimp, garlic, lemon juice, wine, tomatoes, salt, pepper, and cover pot
4. Add 20 coals on top of the lid, bake for 10 minutes until shrimps just cooked enough
5. Serve and enjoy!

For stovetop cooking, the required temperature (approximately) is 300 Degrees F /150 Degrees C For a 10-inch Dutch Oven

Nutritional Values (Per Serving)

Calories: 500; Fat: 21 g; Carbohydrates: 31 g; Protein: 51 g

NEW YORK STRIP STEAK

Servings: 2-3
Cooking Time: 20 minutes
Coal Quantity And Placement: 10 Coals (10 Underneath/ 0 Above)

Ingredients

* 1 tablespoon olive oil
* 2 New York Strip Steaks
* Salt and pepper to taste
* ¼ cup shallots, minced
* 6 ounces/170 grams mushrooms, sliced
* ¼ cup dry white wine
* ¼ cup of water
* ¼ cup sour cream

Method

1. Build a campfire by arranging a bed of coal and letting the fire burn until coals are red hot, 10 coals on bottom
2. Placed Dutch Oven over coal and add oil, let it heat up
3. Season steaks with salt and pepper, add to the pot
4. Cook for 8 minutes, turning once, until medium-rare in the center
5. Drain excess oil from pot, leaving 1 tablespoons oil
6. Add shallots, mushrooms and stir until soft for 8 minutes
7. Add wine and scrape for 2 minutes
8. Add water, sour cream to the pot and cook for 2 minutes until sauce is thick
9. Serve steaks with sauce spooned over the top
10. Enjoy!

For stovetop cooking, the required temperature (approximately) is 200 Degrees F /100 Degrees C For a 10-inch Dutch Oven

Nutritional Values (Per Serving)

Calories: 680; Fat: 3 g; Carbohydrates: 7 g; Protein: 57 g

HEART BEEF STROGANOFF

Servings: 4-6
Cooking Time: 40 minutes
Coal Quantity And Placement: 21 Coals (7 Underneath/ 14 Above)

Ingredients

* 1-pound/0.5kg beef brisket
* 2 white onions, chopped
* 1 tablespoon paprika
* 3 tablespoons balsamic vinegar
* 1 teaspoon chili flakes
* 1 teaspoon cornstarch
* ½ teaspoon ground black pepper
* ½ teaspoon salt
* 2 tablespoons sour cream
* 1 tablespoon sour cream
* 1 tablespoon butter
* 6 ounces/170 grams mushroom, sliced

Method

1. Build a campfire by laying a bed of coals on the ground and allowing the fire to burn until the coals are red hot, about 7 coals on the bottom.
2. In a large mixing bowl, combine the chopped beef brisket, paprika, and balsamic vinegar.
3. Season beef with chili flakes and freshly ground black pepper.
4. Stir in the salt.
5. Allow it to marinate for 10 minutes.
6. Place the Dutch Oven over high heat, add the beef broth, sliced mushrooms, and butter, and bring the liquid to a boil.
7. Toss in the sour cream and beef brisket.
8. Stir in the chopped onion.
9. Add the cornstarch and stir well. Cover and cook for 40 minutes with 14 coals on top.
10. After you've finished, give it a gentle stir and enjoy!

For stovetop cooking, the required temperature (approximately) is 350 Degrees F/175 Degrees C For a 10-inch Dutch Oven

Nutritional Values (Per Serving)

Calories: 190; Fat: 9 g; Carbohydrates: 28 g; Protein: 10 g

PERFECT MONGOLIAN BEEF

Servings: 4-6
Cooking Time: 30 minutes
Coal Quantity And Placement: 21 Coals (7 Underneath/ 14 Above)

Ingredients

* 1-pound/ 0.5kg flank beef steak
* 1 teaspoon fresh ginger
* 1-ounce/28 grams chives
* ½ cup of soy sauce
* ½ cup beef broth
* 1/3 teaspoon sugar
* 1 teaspoon cornstarch
* 1 tablespoon avocado oil
* 1 teaspoon salt

Method

1. Build a campfire by arranging a bed of coal and letting the fire burn until coals are red hot, 7 coals on bottom
2. Add avocado oil to Dutch Oven, place over hot coals, let it heat for 5 minutes
3. Chop flank beefsteak roughly, sprinkle fresh ginger, chives, soy sauce, beef broth, sugar, and stir. Stir in meat and add salt
4. Transfer beef to Dutch Oven and cook for 10 minutes, stirring from time to time
5. Add all remaining liquid and cornstarch
6. Place lid and add 14 coals on top
7. Cook for 30 minutes, stir meat and serve
8. Enjoy!

For stovetop cooking, the required temperature (approximately) is 350 Degrees F/175 Degrees C For a 10-inch Dutch Oven

Nutritional Values (Per Serving)

Calories: 420; Fat: 22 g; Carbohydrates: 14 g; Protein: 36 g

COOL MANGO SHRIMP

Servings: 4
Cooking Time: 10 minutes
Coal Quantity And Placement: 10 Coals (10 Underneath/ 0 Above)

Ingredients

* 2 tablespoons cooking oil
* 1 large onion, chopped
* 2 medium mangoes, cubed
* ¼ cup of soy sauce
* 2 limes, juiced
* 2 pounds/ 1 kg shrimp, peeled and deveined

Method

1. Build a campfire by arranging a bed of coal and letting the fire burn until coals are red hot, 10 coals on bottom
2. Place Dutch Oven over coals and let it heat up
3. Add onion, cook for 5 minutes until tender
4. Add mango, soy sauce, lime juice, shrimp and cook for 5 minutes until shrimps are cooked thoroughly
5. Serve and enjoy!

For stovetop cooking, the required temperature (approximately) is 275 Degrees F/135 Degrees C For a 10-inch Dutch Oven

Nutritional Values (Per Serving)

Calories: 330; Fat: 6 g; Carbohydrates: 47 g; Protein: 22 g

BALSAMIC BRAISED CHICKEN

Servings: 6
Cooking Time: 50 minutes
Coal Quantity And Placement: 14 Coals (14 Underneath/ 0 Above)

Ingredients

* 2 tablespoons cooking oil
* 3 pounds/1.3 kg boneless, skinless chicken thigh
* 1 teaspoon salt
* ¾ teaspoon fresh ground black pepper
* 3 garlic cloves, minced
* 6 ounces/170 grams tomato paste
* ½ cup of water
* 2/3 cup balsamic vinegar
* 3 tablespoons honey

Method

1. Build a campfire by laying a coal bed on the ground and burning until the coals are red hot, with 14 coals on the bottom.
2. Season the chicken with salt and pepper all over, then place it in the Dutch Oven over the coals.
3. Cook the chicken in batches if necessary; it should take about 6 minutes for them to brown.
4. As the chicken browns, remove it from the pot and place it on a plate.
5. Cook for 1 minute, stirring occasionally.
6. Stir in the tomato paste and cook for 2 minutes, stirring constantly.
7. Bring the mixture to a boil with vinegar and honey.
8. Return the chicken to the pot and remove 6 coals from underneath; continue to cook until the chicken is tender and cooked and the sauce has thickened. It should take around 30-40 minutes to complete.
9. Return 6 coals to the bottom of the pan and continue to cook until the sauce is ready.
10. Serve and have fun!

For stovetop cooking, the required temperature (approximately) is 300 Degrees F /150 Degrees C For a 10-inch Dutch Oven

Nutritional Values (Per Serving)

Calories: 680; Fat: 44 g; Carbohydrates: 15 g; Protein: 53 g

CHICKEN BRAISED IN COCONUT MILK AND BASIL

Servings: 6
Cooking Time: 75 minutes
Coal Quantity And Placement: 26 Coals (Follow Procedure For Placement)

Ingredients

* 2 tablespoons cooking oil
* 1 tablespoon butter
* 3 pounds/1.3 kg boneless, skinless thigh
* Salt and pepper to taste
* 8 garlic cloves, peeled and left whole
* 14 ounces/400 grams of coconut milk
* ½ cup fresh basil, chopped

Method

1. Build a campfire by arranging a bed of coal and letting the fire burn until coals are red hot, 14 coals on bottom
2. Place Dutch Oven over coals and let it heat up
3. Season chicken pieces generously with salt, pepper and add them to the pot, browning them in batches. It should take about 6 minutes. Make sure to turn them in once.
4. Transfer chicken pieces to plate as they are browned
5. Add garlic to the pot, cook for 1 minute, add coconut milk and chicken alongside any juice
6. Cover pot, remove 8 coals from the bottom, and place 20 coals on the lid
7. Bake for 1 hour until chicken is fall-apart tender
8. Remove from heat and stir in basil, serve and enjoy!

For stovetop cooking, the required temperature (approximately) is 425 Degrees F/ 220 Degrees C For a 10-inch Dutch Oven

Nutritional Values (Per Serving)

Calories: 380; Fat: 20 g; Carbohydrates: 23 g; Protein: 30 g

PARM CHICKEN

Servings: 6
Cooking Time: 40 minutes
Coal Quantity And Placement: 26 Coals (8 Underneath/ 18 Above)

Ingredients

* 3 tablespoons olive oil
* 1 large egg, beaten
* 4 boneless chicken breast, halves, pounded
* Salt and pepper to taste
* 1 cup seasoned bread crumbs
* 1 and ½ cups of cheese, shredded
* 2 cups marinara sauce

Method

1. Build a campfire by arranging a bed of coal and letting the fire burn until coals are red hot, 8 coals on bottom
2. Take a bowl and whisk in eggs, season chicken pieces generously with salt and pepper
3. Dunk them in egg, and dunk into bread crumbs
4. Place Dutch Oven over coals and let it heat up
5. Add coated chicken pieces to the pot and cook until both sides are golden brown, for 4 minutes per side
6. Transfer to plate
7. Once all pieces are done, remove excess oil from the pot
8. Add half of the marinara sauce, arrange browned chicken pieces on top, sprinkle cheese on top
9. Cover pot and place 18 hot coals on top, bake for 30 minutes until chicken is cooked thoroughly until cheese has melted and sauce is bubbling
10. Serve and enjoy!

For stovetop cooking, the required temperature (approximately) is 400 Degrees F/200 Degrees C For a 10-inch Dutch Oven

Nutritional Values (Per Serving)

Calories: 470; Fat: 13 g; Carbohydrates: 35 g; Protein: 55 g

DELICIOUS GINGER SOY CHICKEN

Servings: 4-6
Cooking Time: 70 minutes
Coal Quantity And Placement: 10 Coals (10 Underneath/ 0 Above)

Ingredients

* 3 pounds/1.3 kg chicken, skin on, bone-in, thighs
* 1 cup of soy sauce
* 3 cups of water
* 1 piece 2 inches ginger, peeled and thinly sliced
* 3 garlic cloves, crushed
* 3 tablespoons sugar

Method

1. Build a campfire by arranging a bed of coal and letting the fire burn until coals are red hot, 10 coals on bottom
2. Add chicken to Dutch Oven, add soy sauce and water, stir well. The water level should be about ¾ way up the sides of chicken
3. Add more water if needed, place Dutch Oven over hot coal and bring to a boil
4. Remove 4-6 coals to bring the water to simmer
5. Stir in ginger, garlic, sugar, and simmer and cook for 45-60 minutes until chicken is tender
6. Once the liquid is thickened, add additional coals as needed to keep the liquid at a simmer
7. Serve and enjoy!

For stovetop cooking, the required temperature (approximately) is 200 Degrees F/100 Degrees C For a 10-inch Dutch Oven

Nutritional Values (Per Serving)

Calories: 508; Fat: 70 g; Carbohydrates: 70 g; Protein: 9 g

CRISPY BEER FISH

Servings: 4
Cooking Time: 10 minutes
Coal Quantity And Placement: 14 Coals (14 Underneath/ 0 Above)

Ingredients

* 4 cups cooking oil
* 12 ounces/340 grams beer
* 2 cups all-purpose flour, divided
* 1/3 teaspoon salt
* 2 pounds/ 1kg cod fillets, cut diagonally into 5x6 inch long strips
* Malt vinegar for serving

Method

1. Build a campfire by arranging a bed of coal and letting the fire burn until coals are red hot, 14 coals on bottom
2. Place Dutch Oven over hot coals
3. Take a bowl and whisk in beer, 1 and ½ cups flour
4. Stir in ½ teaspoon salt
5. Place remaining ½ cup of flour in a wide flat bowl
6. Pat the fish dry with paper towels, season both sides with salt and pepper
7. Dunk each piece of fish in batter, dredge it in flour, lower gently into Dutch Oven
8. Cook several pieces at once
9. Turn the fish pieces frequently; it should take about 5 minutes
10. Season with salt and pepper, transfer towel-lined plate
11. Serve with malt vinegar on top
12. Enjoy!

For stovetop cooking, the required temperature (approximately) is 300 Degrees F/150 Degrees C For a 10-inch Dutch Oven

Nutritional Values (Per Serving)

Calories: 820; Fat: 18 g; Carbohydrates: 80 g; Protein: 6 g

SHRIMP STEW

Servings: 4
Cooking Time: 35 minutes
Coal Quantity And Placement: 21 Coals (7 Underneath/ 14 Above)

Ingredients

* 6 ounces/170 grams green beans
* 10 ounces/280 grams shrimps, peeled
* 1 sweet pepper, chopped
* ½ chili pepper, chopped
* ½ cup half and half
* ½ teaspoon salt
* ½ teaspoon lemongrass
* ½ teaspoon curry powder
* 1 teaspoon palm sugar
* 1 tablespoon fish sauce

Method

1. Build a campfire by arranging a bed of coal and letting the fire burn until coals are red hot, 7 coals on bottom
2. Add green beans to Dutch Oven, add chopped sweet pepper, chili pepper, and fish sauce
3. Add palm sugar, curry powder and stir well
4. Place Dutch Oven over hot coals, cook for 5 minutes, add half and a half and sprinkle lemongrass and cook for 10 minutes more
5. Add peeled shrimps and remaining ingredients
6. Place lid and add 14 coals on top
7. Cook for 20 minutes, serve and enjoy!

For stovetop cooking, the required temperature (approximately) is 350 Degrees F/175 Degrees C For a 10-inch Dutch Oven

Nutritional Values (Per Serving)

Calories: 290; Fat: 17 g; Carbohydrates: 21 g; Protein: 12g

JUICY MEAT CASSEROLE

Servings: 4-6
Cooking Time: 45 minutes
Coal Quantity And Placement: 21 Coals (7 Underneath/ 14 Above)

Ingredients

* 6 ounces/170 grams Monterey Jack Cheese
* 10 ounces/283 grams ground beef
* 1 onion, diced
* 6 ounces/170 grams leek, chopped
* ¼ cup fresh parsley, chopped
* ½ teaspoon salt
* 1 zucchini, grated
* ½ teaspoon chili flakes
* 1 tablespoon olive oil
* ½ cup chicken stock

Method

1. Build a campfire by arranging a bed of coal and letting the fire burn until coals are red hot, 7 coals on bottom
2. Take a bowl and add ground beef, diced onion, chopped leek, chopped parsley, salt, chili flakes, and stir mix
3. Add olive oil to Dutch Oven and place ground beef mixture
4. Add grated zucchini over ground beef, sprinkle chopped cheese
5. Add chicken stock, place lid on top, and add 14 coals on top
6. Cook for 45 minutes
7. Serve and enjoy!

For stovetop cooking, the required temperature (approximately) is 350 Degrees F/175 Degrees C For a 10-inch Dutch Oven

Nutritional Values (Per Serving)

Calories: 820; Fat: 53 g; Carbohydrates: 20 g; Protein: 49 g

CHAPTER 7:
SIDES AND SNACKS RECIPES

MEXICAN BEAN AND RICE

Servings: 6
Cooking Time: 25 minutes
Coal Quantity And Placement: 24 Coals (10 Underneath/ 18 Above, taking 4 from below)

Ingredients

* 1 tablespoon olive oil
* 1 cup long-grain white rice
* 2 teaspoons chili powder
* 1 teaspoon cumin
* 15 ounces/425 grams pinto beans, drained and rinsed
* 1 and ½ cups salsa
* 1 and ½ cups of water
* 1 teaspoon salt
* ½ teaspoon freshly ground pepper

Method

1. Build a campfire by arranging a bed of coal and letting the fire burn until coals are red hot, 10 coals on bottom
2. Place Dutch Oven over hot coal, stir in rice, and cook for 1 minute
3. Add chili powder, cumin, cook for 30 seconds
4. Stir in beans, salsa, pepper
5. Cover Dutch Oven and remove 4 coals from underneath, place 18 coals on top
6. Cook for 20 minutes until rice is tender
7. Serve hot and enjoy!

For stovetop cooking, the required temperature (approximately) is 400 Degrees F/205 Degrees C For a 10-inch Dutch Oven

Nutritional Values (Per Serving)

Calories: 643; Fat: 6 g; Carbohydrates: 21 g; Protein: 21 g

PARM RISOTTO

Servings: 8
Cooking Time: 40 minutes
Coal Quantity And Placement: 25 Coals (8 Underneath/ 17 Above)

Ingredients

* ¼ cup olive oil
* 2 garlic cloves, minced
* 2 cups arborio rice
* 6 cups vegetable broth
* 1 and ¼ cup parmesan cheese, grated
* Salt as needed
* Freshly ground black pepper

Method

1. Build a campfire by arranging a bed of coal and letting the fire burn until coals are red hot, 8 coals on bottom
2. Place Dutch Oven over hot coals let it heat up
3. Add garlic, cook for 1 minute
4. Stir in rice until grains are coated with oil
5. Add broth, cover pot
6. Place 17 coals on top, let it bake for 35 minutes until rice is tender
7. Remove lid and stir in cheese
8. Season with salt and pepper
9. Enjoy!

For stovetop cooking, the required temperature (approximately) is 400 Degrees F/205 Degrees C For a 10-inch Dutch Oven

Nutritional Values (Per Serving)

Calories: 214; Fat: 5 g; Carbohydrates: 25 g; Protein: 7 g

BALSAMIC ROASTED VEGETABLES

Servings: 6
Cooking Time: 40 minutes
Coal Quantity And Placement: 32 Coals (8 Underneath/ 24 Above)

Ingredients

  * 2 tablespoons balsamic vinegar
  * 1 teaspoon Dijon mustard
  * ½ cup olive oil
  * 1 teaspoon salt
  * ½ teaspoon freshly ground black pepper
  * 3 garlic cloves, pressed
  * 2 large red onions, halved and thinly sliced
  * 2 and ¼ pounds/1 kg mixed vegetables, chopped (bell peppers, zucchini, eggplant, etc.)

Method

1. Build a campfire by arranging a bed of coal and letting the fire burn until coals are red hot, 8 coals on bottom
2. Take a medium-sized bowl and whisk in vinegar, mustard
3. Whisk in oil, salt, and pepper
4. Place Dutch Oven over hot coals, add garlic, onion, vegetables
5. Drizzle balsamic mixture over the top, toss well
6. Cover with a lid, add 24 coals to the lid
7. Roast for 30-35 minutes until vegetables are tender, lightly browned
8. Serve and enjoy!

For stovetop cooking, the required temperature (approximately) is 475 Degrees F /250 Degrees C For a 10-inch Dutch Oven

Nutritional Values (Per Serving)

Calories: 644; Fat: 10 g; Carbohydrates: 10 g; Protein: 5 g

CREAMY MASHED POTATOES WITH GREEK YOGURT

Servings: 6
Cooking Time: 35 minutes
Coal Quantity And Placement: 14 Coals (14 Underneath/ 8 Above, taken from bottom)

Ingredients

* 5 pounds/ 2.25 kg red potatoes, quartered
* ¾ cup plain Greek yogurt
* 2 tablespoons unsalted butter
* Salt as needed

Method

1. Build a campfire by arranging a bed of coal and letting the fire burn until coals are red hot, 14 coals on bottom
2. Place Dutch Oven over coals, add water and potatoes
3. Bring to a boil, remove 8 coals from beneath and place it on top of the lid
4. Cook for 30 minutes
5. Remove oven from heat, drain potatoes and return them to pot
6. Mash potatoes with a large fork or potato masher
7. Add butter, mash It into potatoes
8. Stir in yogurt, stir in salt to taste
9. Enjoy!

For stovetop cooking, the required temperature (approximately) is 275 Degrees F /135 Degrees C For a 10-inch Dutch Oven

Nutritional Values (Per Serving)

Calories: 341; Fat: 3 g; Carbohydrates: 23 g; Protein: 9 g

SWEET POTATO FRIES DELIGHT

Servings: 6
Cooking Time: 20 minutes
Coal Quantity And Placement: 16 Coals (16 Underneath/ 0 Above)

Ingredients

* 1 tablespoon chili powder
* 2 teaspoons ground cumin
* 1 teaspoon salt
* 1 teaspoon garlic powder
* 4 cups cooking oil
* 3 medium sweet potatoes, peeled and cut into ¼ inch wide sticks

Method

1. Build a campfire by arranging a bed of coal and letting the fire burn until coals are red hot, 16 coals on bottom
2. Take a small bowl and stir in chili powder, cumin, salt, garlic powder
3. Place Dutch oven over hot coal, add 3 inches oil and let it heat up
4. Drop fries into hot oil and cook until golden brown for 5 minutes; cook in batches if needed
5. Transfer cooked fries to a paper towel, sprinkle spice mix
6. Enjoy!

For stovetop cooking, the required temperature (approximately) is 300 Degrees F/150 Degrees C For a 10-inch Dutch Oven

Nutritional Values (Per Serving)

Calories: 215; Fat: 20 g; Carbohydrates: 25 g; Protein: 5 g

CREAMY POLENTA AND CORN

Servings: 8
Cooking Time: 60 minutes
Coal Quantity And Placement: 24 Coals (6 Underneath/ 18 Above)

Ingredients

* ¼ cup unsalted butter
* 2 cups uncooked polenta
* 2 cups corn kernels, frozen
* 2 teaspoons salt
* 1 teaspoon black pepper
* 1 cup parmesan cheese grated
* 4 ounces/ 112 grams cream cheese

Method

1. Build a campfire by arranging a bed of coal and letting the fire burn until coals are red hot, 6 coals on bottom
2. Place Dutch Oven over coal, add butter, and let it melt
3. Add polenta, corn, salt, and pepper
4. Stir well, place lid on top, and add 18 hot coals on top
5. Bake for 45 minutes
6. Remove lid and stir in parmesan cheese, cream cheese, remaining butter
7. Replace lid and hot coals, bake for 15 minutes
8. Serve and enjoy!

For stovetop cooking, the required temperature (approximately) is 400 Degrees F /205 Degrees C For a 10-inch Dutch Oven

Nutritional Values (Per Serving)

Calories: 152; Fat:10 g; Carbohydrates: 20 g; Protein: 15 g

SWEET AND SAVORY BOURBON BAKED BEANS

Servings: 4
Cooking Time: 85 minutes
Coal Quantity And Placement: 24 Coals (10 Underneath/ 18 Above, take 4 from bottom)

Ingredients

* 4 ounces/ 112 grams thick-cut bacon, diced
* 1 cup brown sugar
* ½ cup spicy mustard
* 1 and ¼ cups of water
* 2/3 cup bourbon
* 45 ounces/ 1275 grams navy beans, drained and rinsed
* Salt as needed
* Pepper as needed

Method

1. Build a campfire by arranging a bed of coal and letting the fire burn until coals are red hot, 10 coals on bottom
2. Place Dutch Oven over coals and let it heat up
3. Add bacon, cook for 6 minutes until browned
4. Transfer bacon to a paper towel-lined plate, drain excess fat
5. Add brown sugar, mustard, water, bourbon to Oven, bring to a boil
6. Keep stirring until sugar dissolves. Stir in beans, salt, pepper, and cover pot
7. Remove 4 coals from the bottom and place 18 coals on top
8. Cook for 45-60 minutes, add more water if needed
9. Add cooked bacon, stir well
10. Cook for 15 minutes more
11. Serve and enjoy!

For stovetop cooking, the required temperature (approximately) is 400 Degrees F/205 Degrees C For a 10-inch Dutch Oven

Nutritional Values (Per Serving)

Calories: 215; Fat: 5 g; Carbohydrates: 14 g; Protein: 6 g

THE GREAT MEAT SAUCE SPAGHETTI

Servings: 4-6
Cooking Time: 40 minutes
Coal Quantity And Placement: 24 Coals (8 Underneath/ 16 Above)

Ingredients

* 1 and ½ pounds/0.6 kg lean beef, ground
* 1 onion, diced
* 1 teaspoon salt
* 2 garlic cloves, minced
* 28 ounces/800 grams Italian diced tomatoes, with herb and juice
* 16 ounces/450 grams package spaghetti, broken in half

Method

1. Build a campfire by arranging a bed of coal and letting the fire burn until coals are red hot, 8 coals on bottom
2. Place Dutch Oven over hot coals, add beef, cook, stirring well, and break up with a spatula
3. Brown the meat and stir in onion, salt, garlic, and cook for 5 minutes until onion is tender
4. Stir in tomatoes, alongside juice. Add spaghetti and bring to a simmer
5. Cover pot with lid and place 16 coals on top.
6. Cook for 20-30 minutes, making sure to check after 15 minutes, add more water if needed
7. Serve once done
8. Enjoy!

For stovetop cooking, the required temperature (approximately) is 375 Degrees F/190 Degrees C For a 10-inch Dutch Oven

Nutritional Values (Per Serving)

Calories: 362; Fat: 16 g; Carbohydrates: 21 g; Protein: 6 g

CHAPTER 8:
BREAD AND ROLLS

EPIC BANANA BREAD

Servings: 18
Cooking Time: 40 minutes
Coal Quantity And Placement: 23 Coals (7 Underneath/ 16 Above)

Ingredients

* 1/2 cup unsalted butter
* 1 cup of sugar
* 4 large eggs, lightly beaten
* 4 large ripe bananas, mashed
* 3 cups all-purpose flour
* 1 tablespoon baking powder
* ¼ teaspoon salt

Method

1. Build a campfire by arranging a bed of coal and letting the fire burn until coals are red hot, 7 coals on bottom
2. Coat Dutch Oven with butter, lightly
3. Take a medium bowl and stir in butter, sugar, eggs, bananas and stir well
4. Add flour, baking powder, salt, and stir well
5. Transfer batter to Dutch Oven
6. Place oven over hot coals, place lid, add 16 coals on top, making sure to turn the pot every 15 minutes
7. Bake for 40 minutes
8. Once the bread is ready, let it rest for 5-10 minutes, serve and enjoy!

For stovetop cooking, the required temperature (approximately) is 375 Degrees F/190 Degrees C For a 10-inch Dutch Oven

Nutritional Values (Per Serving)

Calories: 631; Fat: 4 g; Carbohydrates: 15 g; Protein: 10 g

BUTTERED UP BEER BREAD

Servings: 18
Cooking Time: 60 minutes
Coal Quantity And Placement: 21 Coals (7 Underneath/ 14 Above)

Ingredients

* 6 tablespoons melted unsalted butter
* 4 and ½ cups self-rising flour
* 5 tablespoons sugar
* ½ teaspoon salt
* 12 ounces/340 grams beer

Method

1. Build a campfire by arranging a bed of coal and letting the fire burn until coals are red hot, 7 coals on bottom
2. Coat Dutch Oven lightly with butter, place it over coals
3. Take a large-sized bowl and mix in flour, sugar, salt
4. Stir in beer until mixed well, remove Dutch Oven from heat
5. Transfer dough into it, cover the pot, and let the dough rise for 20 minutes
6. Drizzle melted butter on top of the dough, cover the pot
7. Place 14 coals on top and cook for 15-20 minutes, making sure to rotate the lid by a quarter every 10 minutes
8. Take the pot off coals, leaving coals on top, let it cook for 40 minutes more until bread is golden brown
9. Serve and enjoy!

For stovetop cooking, the required temperature (approximately) is 375 Degrees F /190 Degrees C For a 10-inch Dutch Oven

Nutritional Values (Per Serving)

Calories: 256; Fat: 35 g; Carbohydrates: 20 g; Protein: 6 g

HONEY-SWEETENED CORNBREAD

Servings: 8
Cooking Time: 25 minutes
Coal Quantity And Placement: 25 Coals (8 Underneath/ 17 Above)

Ingredients

* 6 tablespoon melted butter
* 1 and ½ cups cornmeal
* 1 and ½ cups + 1 tablespoon self-rising flour
* 1 teaspoon salt
* 3 large eggs, beaten
* 1 and ½ milk or buttermilk
* ½ cup honey

Method

1. Build a campfire by arranging a coal bed and letting the fire burn until the coals are red hot, with 8 coals on the bottom.
2. Place Dutch Oven over coals. Place lid and place 17 hot coals on top.
3. Take a large bowl, whisk in cornmeal, flour, salt. Take a medium-sized bowl and whisk in eggs, buttermilk, honey, melted butter until combined well
4. Add egg mixture to dry ingredients, stir well
5. Remove oven from heat, pour batter into the pan, spreading it out evenly
6. Replace lid with coals on top, bake for 25 minutes until a toothpick into center comes clean
7. Serve and enjoy!

For stovetop cooking, the required temperature (approximately) is 400 Degrees F/205 Degrees C For a 10-inch Dutch Oven

Nutritional Values (Per Serving)

Calories: 442; Fat: 21 g; Carbohydrates: 31 g; Protein: 5 g

NUTELLA FLAVORED BROWNIES

Servings: 8
Cooking Time: 50 minutes
Coal Quantity And Placement: 21 Coals (7 Underneath/ 14 Above)

Ingredients

* 1 cup of sugar
* 3 large eggs
* 1 cup all-purpose flour
* ½ cup Dutch cocoa powder
* ½ teaspoon salt
* ½ teaspoon vanilla extract
* ½ stick unsalted butter
* ¼ cup half and half
* 4 ounces/112 grams chocolate chip
* ½ cup Nutella spread

Method

1. Build a campfire by arranging a bed of coal and letting the fire burn until coals are red hot, with 7 coals on the bottom.
2. Take a bowl and whisk in sugar and eggs
3. Whisk flour, cocoa, salt in another bowl
4. Place Dutch Oven over coals and add butter, let it simmer, add half and a half and stir well
5. Add chocolate chips and stir for 2 minutes until melted well
6. Add Nutella, stir until mixed
7. Remove heat
8. Add sugar mixture into the chocolate mix in Dutch Oven
9. Add flour mix and fold well until incorporated
10. Place lid and add 14 coals on top, bake for 25 minutes making sure to check after 20 minutes using a toothpick for consistency
11. Serve once done; enjoy!

For stovetop cooking, the required temperature (approximately) is 350 Degrees F/175 Degrees C For a 10-inch Dutch Oven

Nutritional Values (Per Serving)

Calories: 23; Fat: 25 g; Carbohydrates: 10 g; Protein: 6 g

POTATO BALLS

Servings: 4
Cooking Time: 10 minutes
Coal Quantity And Placement: 21 Coals (7 Underneath/ 14 Above)

Ingredients

*   7 ounces/200 grams potato, mashed
*   1 tablespoon flour
*   14 cup panko breadcrumbs
*   2 whole eggs, whisked
*   1 teaspoon dried dill
*   ½ teaspoon salt
*   2 tablespoon olive oil
*   1 teaspoon paprika

Method

1. Build a campfire by arranging a bed of coal and letting the fire burn until coals are red hot, with 7 coals on the bottom.
2. Take a bowl and mix in mashed potatoes, flour
3. Add whisked eggs, dried dill, season with salt and pepper
4. Mix well until smooth
5. Make medium sized balls from potato mixture and coat them into panko breadcrumbs
6. Add olive oil to Dutch Oven, place it over hot coal
7. Let it heat up, add potato balls and place the lid
8. Place 14 coals on top and cook for 10 minutes
9. Once the balls the light brown, serve and enjoy!

For stovetop cooking, the required temperature (approximately) is 350 Degrees F/180 Degrees C For a 10-inch Dutch Oven

Nutritional Values (Per Serving)

Calories: 233; Fat: 9 g; Carbohydrates: 24 g; Protein: 15 g

CINNAMON AND RAISIN BREAD PUDDING

Servings: 4-5
Cooking Time: 45 minutes
Coal Quantity And Placement: 24 Coals (10 Underneath/ 14 Above)

Ingredients

* ½ cup unsalted butter
* 4 cups whole milk
* 8 large eggs
* ¼ cup brown sugar
* 2 teaspoons vanilla extract
* 1 pound/ 0.5kg cinnamon raisin bread, cut into cubes

Method

1. Make a campfire by arranging a bed of coals and allowing the fire to burn until the coals are red hot about 10 coals.
2. Heat the Dutch oven and add the butter, allowing it to melt.
3. Remove from the heat and stir in the milk, eggs, brown sugar, and vanilla extract.
4. Whisk thoroughly, then fold in the cubed bread until evenly coated.
5. Place 14 coals on top of the oven and cover it.
6. Bake for 45 minutes or until the mixture is firm.
7. Serve and have fun!

Nutritional Values (Per Serving)

Calories: 421; Fat: 23 g; Carbohydrates: 2 g; Protein: 8 g

ORIGINAL MEATLOAF

Servings: 4-6
Cooking Time: 60 minutes
Coal Quantity And Placement: 24 Coals (9 Underneath/ 15 Above, take 3 from the bottom when needed)

Ingredients

* 1 tablespoon cooking oil
* 1 and ½ pounds/0.7 kg lean ground beef
* 1 teaspoon salt
* ½ teaspoon fresh ground black pepper
* ½ onion, finely minced
* 1 large egg, beaten
* ½ cup bread crumbs
* ¾ cup ketchup, divided

Method

1. Build a campfire by arranging a bed of coal and letting the fire burn until coals are red hot; 9 coals on bottom
2. Coat bottom of Dutch Oven with oil, if using tin foil, layer on the bottom of Dutch Ovens and coat with a light layer of oil
3. Take a large bowl and mix in beef, salt, pepper, onion, egg, bread crumbs, ¼ cup of ketchup
4. Transfer mixture to Dutch oven and form into a flat, round loaf in the center of the pot, with space around sides
5. Cover top of meatloaf with ½ cup ketchup
6. Cover pot, and place it over coal
7. Place 15 coals on the lid on top
8. Cook for 45-60 minutes until ready. Remove heat and let it stand for 5-10 minutes, slice, and enjoy!

For stovetop cooking, the required temperature (approximately) is 375 Degrees F/190 Degrees C For a 10-inch Dutch Oven

Nutritional Values (Per Serving)

Calories: 222; Fat: 6 g; Carbohydrates: 25 g; Protein: 10 g

EFFICIENT NO-KNEAD GOURMET BREAD

Servings: 4-6
Cooking Time: 40-60 minutes

Ingredients

3 cups all-purpose flour
2 teaspoon salt
1 teaspoon active dry yeast
1 teaspoon fresh rosemary, chopped
1 and 2/3 cups warm water (at 110 degrees F)
1 teaspoon fresh sage, chopped
1 teaspoon fresh thyme, chopped

Method

1. Add flour, salt, and yeast in a large-sized bowl
2. Mix well
3. Add water and herbs and mix again until incorporated
4. Cover the bowl with plastic wrap and let it sit for 18-24 hours
5. Flour and prepare your workspace
6. Once the dough has risen, transfer the dough to your workplace and dust it with flour
7. Fold dough in half and form a nice ball, stretching and tucking the edges methodically
8. Flour a kitchen towel and place the dough ball on your floured towel
9. Cover with another towel
10. Let the dough rise for 2 hours more
11. Preheat your oven to 450 degrees F
12. Transfer a lidded Dutch Oven to your oven, let it pre-heat
13. Remove hot Dutch Oven from oven and remove the lid
14. Carefully turn the dough ball into your Dutch Oven (seam side up)
15. Shake the dough to ensure that it is distributed evenly
16. Cover with lid and bake for 30 minutes
17. Remove lid and bake for 15-20 minutes more
18. Remove loaf from the dish and let it cool
19. Slice and serve
20. Enjoy!

Nutritional Values (Per Serving)

Calories: 422; Fat: 12 g; Carbohydrates: 23 g; Protein: 6 g

DELICIOUS AND SATISFYING PIZZA

Servings: 4-6
Cooking Time: 30 minutes

Ingredients

For Pizza Dough
* 4 and ½ cups bread flour
* 1 tablespoon salt
* ½ tablespoon granulated sugar
* 1 envelope (7g) instant dry yeast
* 15 ounces lukewarm water
* 3 tablespoons olive oil, more for brushing

Toppings
* 8-10 ounces whole mozzarella, sliced up into ½ inch cubes
* Toppings such as olives, prosciutto, mushrooms, etc.
* Fresh basil, chopped
* Fresh parmesan, grated

For Pizza Sauce
* fresh ground black pepper
* pinch of granulated sugar
* 2 teaspoons olive oil
* 2 clove garlic, grated
* 1 teaspoon salt
* 1 can (15 ounces) tomatoes, drained

Method

For Dough
1. Take a bowl and use an electric mixer (fitted with paddle attachment), and whisk flour, salt, yeast, and sugar
2. Add olive oil, water, and mix until fully incorporated (try using the hook attachment)
3. Keep mixing the dough until it becomes smooth, take it out, and transfer to a lightly floured surface
4. Keep kneading by hand for a few minutes
5. Divide the dough into three equal pieces (about 12-13 ounces each) and form balls
6. Transfer to a baking tray and lightly brush with olive oil
7. Cover with plastic wrap and transfer to a warm spot
8. Let it rise for 1 and ½ hours

For Sauce
9. Take your blender jar and add drained tomatoes, puree
10. Transfer the pureed tomatoes to a bowl
11. Stir in grated garlic, olive oil, salt, sugar, pepper

12. Keep it on the side and let it refrigerate until needed
13. Making Pizza
14. Preheat your oven to 450 degrees F, keeping your Dutch Oven on the lowest part of the oven
15. Once the dough has doubled in size, roll dough on a lightly floured surface and roll it out into a disk of 12 inches wide
16. Once the dough does not bounce back anymore, let it rest for a while
17. Transfer prepared dough to a piece of parchment paper and let it rest for a few minutes
18. Lightly brush dough with olive oil
19. Spread a third of your sauce in a thin layer

Top with your desired toppings

20. Take a small paddle and bring pizza to your Dutch Oven
21. Bake for 12-15 minutes until the crust shows a golden texture and the cheese melts
22. Remove the Dutch Oven from the oven and use parchment paper to carefully lift out the pizza to your cutting board
23. Slice and enjoy!
24. Repeat for the remaining pizzas!

Nutritional Values (Per Serving)

Calories: 256; Fat: 14 g; Carbohydrates: 5 g; Protein: 8 g

CHAPTER 9:
DESSERT RECIPES

CINNAMON DRESSED RICE PUDDING

Servings: 8
Cooking Time: 50 minutes
Coal Quantity And Placement: 21 Coals (7 Underneath/ 14 Above)

Ingredients

* 1 tablespoon butter
* 2 cups cooked white rice
* ½ teaspoon cinnamon, ground
* ¾ cup of sugar
* 5 large eggs, beaten
* 2 cups heavy cream
* 1 teaspoon vanilla extract
* Sprinkle of ground cinnamon

Method

1. Build a campfire by arranging a bed of coal and letting the fire burn until coals are red hot, with 7 coals on the bottom.
2. Take your Dutch Oven and butter the inside, add butter and put rice
3. Take a large bowl and mix in cinnamon, sugar, eggs and blend well
4. Whisk in cream, vanilla
5. Pour the mixture gently over rice and cover the lid
6. Place it Dutch Oven over a bed of coals and put 14 coals on top, let it bake for 50 minutes
7. Serve and enjoy with a sprinkle of cinnamon!

For stovetop cooking, the required temperature (approximately) is 350 Degrees F/175 Degrees C For a 10-inch Dutch Oven

Nutritional Values (Per Serving)

Calories: 110; Fat: 2 g; Carbohydrates: 20 g; Protein: 3 g

BANANA CLAFOUTI

Servings: 8
Cooking Time: 45 minutes
Coal Quantity And Placement: 21 Coals (7 Underneath/ 14 Above)

Ingredients

* 1 cup whole milk
* ¼ cup whipping cream
* 3 whole eggs
* ½ cup sugar, granulated
* 1 teaspoon extract
* 2 tablespoons butter, melted
* ¼ teaspoon salt
* ½ cup all-purpose flour
* 2 bananas, peeled and thinly sliced
* 2 teaspoons fresh lemon juice

Method

1. Build campfire by arranging a coal bed and letting the fire burn until coals are red hot, 7 coals on bottom.
2. Take a bowl and whisk in milk, cream, eggs, sugar, extract, butter, salt
3. Add flour and gently keep whisking it until fully incorporated
4. Place sliced bananas in a bowl with lemon juice
5. Lightly grease Dutch Oven and place it over coals, let it heat for 5 minutes
6. Remove and pour the batter
7. Scatter bananas over batter and return to coal, place lid on top and add 14 coals on top
8. Bake for 35 minutes
9. Serve and enjoy!

For stovetop cooking, the required temperature (approximately) is 350 Degrees F/175 Degrees C For a 10-inch Dutch Oven

Nutritional Values (Per Serving)

Calories: 860; Fat: 4 g; Carbohydrates: 27 g; Protein: 2 g

THE DOUBLE-DISH GIANT CHOCOLATE CHIP COOKIE

Servings: 6
Cooking Time: 30 minutes
Coal Quantity And Placement: 21 Coals (7 Underneath/ 14 Above)

Ingredients

* ½ cup unsalted butter
* ½ cup light brown sugar
* ½ cup white sugar
* 1 teaspoon vanilla
* 1 large egg
* 1 cup all-purpose flour
* ½ teaspoon salt
* 1 cup chocolate chip
* ½ cups chocolate chip chunks

Method

1. Build campfire by arranging a coal bed and letting the fire burn until coals are red hot, 7 coals on bottom.
2. Place your Dutch Oven over hot coals and add butter, let it melt
3. Add sugar and stir well
4. Add vanilla, egg and beat quickly to ensure that eggs do not get cooked
5. Stir in flour, baking soda, salt
6. Fold in chocolate chips and chunks and stir until you have a nice dough
7. Spread the dough lightly all over
8. Place lid on top and place 14 coals on top
9. Bake for 25 minutes until cookie appears brown
10. Serve and enjoy!

For stovetop cooking, the required temperature (approximately) is 350 Degrees F /175 Degrees C For a 10-inch Dutch Oven

Nutritional Values (Per Serving)

Calories: 445; Fat: 22 g; Carbohydrates: 55 g; Protein: 10 g

DELICIOUS SWEET CHERRY CLAFOUTI

Servings: 8
Cooking Time: 45 minutes
Coal Quantity And Placement: 21 Coals (7 Underneath/ 14 Above)

Ingredients

* 1 cup whole milk
* ¼ cup whipping cream
* 3 whole eggs
* ½ cup granulated sugar
* 1 teaspoon almond extract
* 2 tablespoons butter, melted
* ½ cup all-purpose flour
* 2 cups cherries, pitted and sliced
* Powdered sugar

Method

1. Build campfire by arranging a coal bed and letting the fire burn until coals are red hot, 7 coals on bottom.
2. Take a bowl and whisk in milk, cream, eggs, sugar, extract, and butter
3. Add flour, whisk well
4. Lightly grease your Dutch Oven, place it overheats, let it heat up for 5 minutes
5. Remove heat and add batter, scatter cherries all around batter
6. Place oven over hot coal, place lid, and add 14 coals on top
7. Bake for 35 minutes until the dish is golden and puffed
8. Dust with powdered sugar, serve and enjoy!

For stovetop cooking, the required temperature (approximately) is 350 Degrees F/175 Degrees C For a 10-inch Dutch Oven

Nutritional Values (Per Serving)

Calories: 200; Fat: 49 g; Carbohydrates: 49 g; Protein: 5 g

JUICY BAKED APPLE DUMPLINGS

Servings: 4
Prep Time: 10 Minutes
Cooking Time: 15 minutes

Ingredients

* 4 Granny Smith apples, peeled and cored
* 1 cup (2 sticks) unsalted butter, at room temperature
* 1/2 cup packed brown sugar
* 1 teaspoon ground cinnamon
* ½ teaspoon ground nutmeg
* 1 sheet puff pastry
* 4 teaspoons granulated sugar
* 1 cup vanilla ice cream

Method

1. Preheat the oven to 400°F. Line the bottom of a Dutch oven with parchment paper and set it aside.
2. Stir together the butter, brown sugar, cinnamon, and nutmeg in a small bowl until well combined.
3. On a clean work surface, unfold the puff pastry and cut it into 4 equal pieces. Place a single apple onto each piece of puff pastry, positioning it in the middle.
4. Divide the butter mixture into 4 equal portions, then lightly coat the outside of each apple with the mixture and stuff at least 1 teaspoon of the mixture inside each apple.
5. Pull the sides of the puff pastry up and over the sides and top of the apple. Crimp the edges, so the pastry completely encloses the apple. Place the covered apples into the prepared Dutch oven, making sure they are evenly spaced with at least 2 inches between them.
6. Sprinkle the top of each apple with 1 teaspoon of granulated sugar.
7. Bake, uncovered, for 25 minutes, or until the pastry is golden brown. Remove and let the rest of the apple for 10 minutes before serving with a scoop of vanilla ice cream and a drizzle of caramel syrup over the top.

Nutritional Values (Per Serving)

Calories: 440; Fat: 20 g; Carbohydrates: 50 g; Protein: 3 g

AWESOME CARAMEL PECAN BARS

Servings: 6
Cooking Time: 35 minutes

Ingredients

* 1 cup all-purpose flour 1A cup sugar
* 1 teaspoon baking powder V2 teaspoon salt
* ½ cup heavy (whipping) cream 8 tablespoons (1 stick) unsalted butter, melted
* 2 large eggs
* 1 teaspoon vanilla extract
* Vz cup pecan pieces
* 12 caramel candies, cut into small pieces Va cup caramel syrup (optional)

Method

1. Preheat the oven to 3 75 °F. Line a Dutch oven with parchment paper and lightly spray it with nonstick cooking spray.
2. In a large bowl, whisk the flour, sugar, baking powder, and salt to combine.
3. Whisk the heavy cream, melted butter, eggs, and vanilla in a small bowl until combined. Stir the wet ingredients into the dry ingredients, then fold in the pecans and caramel candies. Transfer the batter to the prepared Dutch oven.
4. Bake, uncovered, for 3 5 minutes, or until a toothpick inserted in the center comes out clean.

Nutritional Values (Per Serving)

Calories: 900; Fat: 114 g; Carbohydrates: 47 g; Protein: 9 g

THE PERFECT CHERRY DUMP CAKE

Servings: 8
Cooking Time: 50 minutes

Ingredients

* 1/4 cups unsalted butter, at room temperature
* 3 large eggs
* 1 tablespoon vanilla extract
* 1 cup whole milk
* 1/4 cup heavy (whipping) cream
* 1/4 cups all-purpose flour
* 1 cup granulated sugar
* 1 tablespoon baking powder
* 1 teaspoon salt

Method

1. Preheat the oven to 350 ° F. Coat a Dutch oven with nonstick cooking spray and set aside.
2. Using a handheld mixer, beat together the butter, eggs, and vanilla in a large bowl, then stir in the milk and heavy cream until combined.
3. Sift in the flour, granulated sugar, baking powder, and salt and mix until just combined. Spread the pie filling in the Dutch oven, then top with the cake batter. Stir the mixture together slightly, so it is not completely incorporated but swirled.
4. Cover the pot and bake for 30 minutes. Remove the lid and bake for 20 minutes, or until browned on top.
5. Serve hot with a dusting of powdered sugar.

Nutritional Values (Per Serving)

Calories: 306; Fat: 12 g; Carbohydrates: 25 g; Protein: 17 g

CRISPY BERRY CRISP

Servings: 8
Cooking Time: 35 minutes

Ingredients

* 8 tablespoons (1 stick) unsalted butter plus 1 tablespoon
* 2 cups strawberries
* 1 cup blueberries
* cup blackberries
* 1/2 cup raspberries
* ½ tablespoons cornstarch
* 1/4 cup granulated sugar
* 1/4 teaspoon nutmeg
* Grated zest of 1 lemon
* 2 tablespoons freshly squeezed lemon juice
* 1 cup all-purpose flour
* ¼ cup rolled oats
* ¼ cup packed brown sugar
* ½ teaspoon salt

Method

1. Preheat the oven to 400°F. Use 1 tablespoon of butter to lightly coat the bottom and sides of a 5-quart Dutch oven.
2. In the prepared Dutch oven, stir together the strawberries, blueberries, blackberries, raspberries, cornstarch, granulated sugar, nutmeg, lemon zest, and lemon juice until the berries are coated well.
3. Stir together the flour, oats, brown sugar, and salt until combined in a large bowl. Using a fork, blend in the remaining 8 tablespoons (1 stick) of butter until a crumbly mixture forms. Pour the crumble over the berries.
4. Bake, uncovered, for 3 5 minutes, or until the berries are bubbling and
5. the crumble is golden brown. Serve warm.

Nutritional Values (Per Serving)

Calories: 200; Fat: 6 g; Carbohydrates: 105 g; Protein: 39 g

THE PERFECT TRIPPLE LAYER CHOCOLATE CAKE

Servings: 8
Cooking Time: 15 minutes

Ingredients

* 2 cups sugar
* 1/2 cups all-purpose flour
* 3/4 cup unsweetened cocoa powder, plus more for dusting
* 2 teaspoons baking powder
* 1 teaspoon salt
* 1/2 teaspoon ground cinnamon
* 1 cup whole milk
* ½ cup vegetable oil
* ½ cup brewed coffee
* ½ cup heavy (whipping) cream
* 3 large eggs
* 1 tablespoon vanilla extract
* ¼ cup semisweet chocolate chips, melted
* ¼ cup milk chocolate chips, melted

Method

1. Preheat the oven to 3 5 0 ° F. Line a Dutch oven with parchment paper, then lightly coat it with nonstick cooking spray.
2. Sift together the sugar, flour, cocoa powder, baking powder, salt, and cinnamon in a large bowl.
3. Whisk the milk, oil, coffee, heavy cream, eggs, and vanilla to blend in a medium bowl. Add the milk mixture to the dry mixture a little at a time, stirring until just combined.
4. Mix the melted semisweet chocolate and milk chocolate, then transfer the batter to the prepared Dutch oven.
5. Cover the pot and bake for 30 minutes. Remove the lid and bake for 20 minutes, or until a toothpick inserted in the center comes out clean. Serve hot with a dusting of unsweetened cocoa powder.

Nutritional Values (Per Serving)

Calories: 300; Fat: 16 g; Carbohydrates: 30 g; Protein: 4 g

ROASTED APPLE AND SAVORY PORRIDGE DELIGHT

Servings: 4
Cooking Time: 2 hours 30 minutes

Ingredients

* 1 and ½ cups white wine vinegar
* 1 and ½ teaspoons fresh ground pepper
* 1 and ¾ teaspoons kosher salt
* 2 medium Chioggia radicchio, chopped
* 5 sprigs parsley + ½ cup extra chopped parsley
* 3 sprigs thyme
* 1 bay leaf
* 2 garlic cloves, peeled
* 4 small shallots, peeled
* 1 cup spelt
* 1 cup sorghum
* 3 ounces prosciutto, thickly sliced
* 3 quarts sodium chicken broth
* 2 pink lady apples, cut into ½ inch wedges
* 2 tablespoons olive oil
* 2 ounces parmesan, grated
* ½ cup heavy cream
* 1 and ½ cups whole milk

Method

1. Take a medium bowl and whisk in 1 teaspoon salt, 1 teaspoon pepper, 1 cup of water
2. Add radicchio, cover the mixture and let it sit until your dish is ready
3. Tie parsley sprigs, thyme sprigs, and bay leaf together using a kitchen twine
4. Add herb bundle, garlic, shallot, sorghum, spelt, broth, and about 2 cups water to a large-sized pot
5. Bring the mixture to boil over high heat
6. Lower down the heat to low and simmer for 1 and ½- 2 hours until grains are tender and most of the liquid is gone
7. Preheat your oven to 450 degrees F
8. Prepare a rimmed baking sheet and line it with parchment paper
9. Arrange speck on a baking sheet and bake for 5-8 minutes until crispy
10. Let it cool and break it down into medium-sized portions
11. Add apples, oil, ½ teaspoon pepper, ¾ teaspoon salt on another similar pre-

pared rimmed baking sheet and bakeapples for 13-15 minutes

12. Discard the herb bundle from grains
13. Stir in milk, cream and bring the mix to a boil
14. Remove heat and blend the mixture using an immersion blender
15. Once the porridge is thick and creamy, add cheese and keep stirring until melted
16. Season with more salt and pepper accordingly
17. Drain radicchio and add them to a medium bowl alongside chopped parsley
18. Season with salt and pepper
19. Serve porridge in serving bowls with a topping of roasted apple, speck, and pickled radicchio
20. Enjoy!

Nutritional Values (Per Serving)

Calories: 340; Fat: 9 g; Carbohydrates: 26 g; Protein: 10 g

CONCLUSION

Following your first few attempts at some of the recipes in this book, you will quickly realize how simple and enjoyable it is to incorporate simple Dutch Oven meals into your life regularly, particularly with the assistance of a Dutch oven. The dishes in this book range from simple to elegant. There is something for everyone's taste and occasion in this collection. With a Dutch oven, you have now begun your introduction to the simplified and delicious world of limited cooking ingredients, which will continue throughout the rest of this chapter. The days of avoiding the kitchen because you were afraid of being trapped in it all day are long gone.

Now that you are familiar with the Dutch oven techniques, you can move on to the next step and experiment with different flavors and textures. Create your own recipes and keep an open mind when you're grocery shopping. Allow the changing of the seasons to guide your culinary choices. When you pay attention to the natural characteristics and flavors of healthy ingredients, you will notice that they seem to work well together. You will be able to create quick and delicious meals on the fly as a result. Most of the time, the simplest meals are the most delicious, not only because they bring out the most natural flavors but also because you get to enjoy yourself while you're putting together the meal.

Even though cooking with fewer ingredients is not a new concept, doing so is a wise choice because it allows you to recreate the magic of complex and time-consuming kitchens with less effort by throwing the right combination of ingredients into your Dutch oven. For situations where you only have a few contents to work with, you can plan ahead of time and stock your closet with these essential ingredients. When the majority of the ingredients are already prepared and waiting to be used, cooking becomes extremely smooth and simple.

When you're stuck in the daily grind of relaxation, electronics, and obligations, camping can be a welcome respite from your routine. Getting out into nature and breathing in some fresh air can be extremely therapeutic.

With this book, we hope you will be able to take your outdoor enjoyment to the next level by preparing simple meals over a campfire or charcoal grill in the field. If your children have never enjoyed a simple and nutritious meal made with little grass or twigs, now is the time to introduce them to the concept. There is something here for even the most affluent diners, and you will not be disappointed if you try outdoor cooking!

I hope that this book has opened your eyes to the countless possibilities for preparing simple meals in your Dutch oven. It is now your responsibility to take action. Get started on preparing as many of the recipes that we've discussed as you can.

THANK YOU SO MUCH FOR READING THIS BOOK, AND I HOPE YOU START AN ENJOYABLE FOOD JOURNEY RIGHT AWAY!

Made in the USA
Las Vegas, NV
29 November 2023